MW01489928

The Complete USA State ID Checking Guide Book 2024

The Ultimate Reference for ID Verification

Frank Charleston

DISCLAIMER

While every precaution has been taken in the preparation of this book, the publisher assumes no responsibility for errors or omissions, or for damages resulting from the use of the information contained herein.

The Complete USA State ID Checking Guide Book 2024: The Ultimate Reference for ID Verification

First edition.

TABLE OF CONTENTS

PART 1

Introduction to ID Verification

INTRODUCTION

IMPORTANCE OF ACCURATE ID VERIFICATION

Accurate ID verification is a cornerstone of many industries and institutions, serving as a crucial layer of security in daily transactions and operations. Whether it's verifying the age of a customer purchasing alcohol, ensuring the identity of someone boarding a flight, or confirming the legitimacy of a financial transaction, proper ID checks are essential in safeguarding against fraud, illegal activities, and human error. Given the diverse uses of identification across the United States, the importance of performing this task with precision cannot be overstated. The consequences of lax ID verification can range from immediate legal repercussions to long-term reputational damage and financial loss. To understand why accurate ID verification is so important, it's essential to explore its role in various sectors, the risks associated with mistakes, and the evolving landscape of ID security.

One of the most prominent areas where ID verification plays a key role is in the sale of age-restricted products such as alcohol, tobacco, and firearms. Retailers and businesses are legally obligated to ensure that customers meet the age requirements before completing such transactions. Mistakes in this area can lead to significant penalties, including hefty fines, the suspension or revocation of business licenses, and even criminal charges. Beyond the legal ramifications, businesses can suffer severe reputational harm if they are found to have sold restricted products to minors. This is why thorough and accurate ID checks are not just advisable but mandatory. In some cases, even the smallest oversight, such as misreading an expiration date or overlooking a minor discrepancy in the ID's format, can lead to a costly mistake.

Airports and transportation hubs rely heavily on ID verification to maintain security. Given the heightened risks associated with air travel, identity verification ensures that passengers are who they claim to be and that no unauthorized individuals gain access to restricted areas or board flights under false pretenses. The Transportation Security Administration (TSA) and airport staff must adhere to strict ID verification protocols to prevent fraud, terrorism, and other security breaches. Even a single misstep in this process can have dire consequences, potentially compromising the safety of hundreds of passengers. As the REAL ID Act continues to be enforced, understanding the differences between compliant and non-compliant IDs becomes even more critical for both passengers and those responsible for checking identification at checkpoints. This is why airport security personnel must be trained in spotting common errors, identifying fake IDs, and understanding the nuances between various state-issued identification cards.

In the realm of financial services, accurate ID verification is a linchpin in preventing identity theft, fraud, and money laundering. Banks, credit unions, and other financial institutions are required by law to follow Know Your Customer (KYC) regulations, which include the proper verification of identity documents before opening accounts, approving loans, or processing large transactions. Failing to properly verify a customer's identity can lead to the institution inadvertently facilitating fraudulent activity or being used as a conduit for illicit financial transactions. Inaccurate ID checks in financial services can have a ripple effect, leading not only to financial loss for the institution but also to widespread distrust among customers. The rise of identity theft and increasingly sophisticated fraudulent schemes have made this task even more challenging, making it essential for institutions to use the latest verification tools and methods, such as biometric scans, encrypted mobile IDs, and high-tech ID scanners. This ties into the earlier section on technological advances in ID verification, which highlight the importance of staying up-to-date with the latest tools and strategies to combat emerging threats.

Casinos and gambling establishments are another sector where ID verification is paramount. These businesses must verify the age and identity of their customers before allowing them to participate in gambling activities. In addition, casinos often deal with large sums of money and are prime targets for money laundering schemes. Consequently, failing to properly verify IDs can expose the establishment to criminal activities, regulatory fines, and loss of their gambling licenses. Moreover, like in the financial sector, the reputation of a casino can be severely damaged if it becomes known for lax ID checks, making it a target for fraudsters. In high-stakes environments like these, the stakes for accurate ID verification are particularly high. ID scanners, UV light checks, and other advanced tools can be useful here, but so too is the knowledge and expertise of those responsible for verifying IDs.

Hospitality industries such as hotels, rental companies, and short-term lodging services also face significant risks when it comes to ID verification. Ensuring that guests are who they claim to be is crucial for security and legal compliance. Inaccurate or careless ID checks can result in unauthorized individuals gaining access to hotel rooms, rental properties, or vehicles, leading to property damage, theft, and legal issues. In some instances, a fraudulent ID could be used to cover the identity of someone involved in criminal activities, making the business vulnerable to liability claims. As mentioned earlier, technological advancements have made it easier to catch many forms of ID tampering, but businesses must remain vigilant in properly training their staff on how to recognize subtle signs of a fake or tampered ID. Combining human expertise with advanced ID verification tools creates the strongest defense against such risks.

Legal compliance is another reason why accurate ID verification is so critical. Federal and state laws require businesses and institutions to verify identification in a wide variety of contexts, from hiring employees to issuing government benefits. Employers, for instance, must ensure that they properly verify employees' work eligibility, as mandated by U.S. law. Failing to do so can result in severe fines, penalties, and the risk of being charged with employing undocumented workers. Similarly, government agencies that distribute benefits like Social Security, unemployment, or healthcare must conduct thorough ID verification to ensure that benefits are only going to those who are eligible. Falsified or inaccurate ID checks in these contexts not only strain public resources but also undermine the public's trust in these institutions. Understanding the legal requirements for ID verification, as discussed in the section on federal and state laws, is essential for any entity engaging in activities that require identity verification.

Ultimately, the consequences of inaccurate ID verification are not limited to legal and financial penalties but extend to the ethical responsibilities of businesses and institutions. Properly verifying someone's identity ensures that services are only provided to those who are entitled to receive them. Failing to do so not only opens the door to fraud but also can lead to discriminatory practices. For example, if staff are not trained properly in identifying IDs from various states, there is a risk that individuals with out-of-state or non-traditional IDs might be unfairly denied service. This highlights the importance of a thorough understanding of state-specific ID formats, as discussed in the state-by-state guide. Proper ID verification processes ensure fairness and consistency in how individuals are treated, which reinforces trust in the institutions responsible for these checks.

Accurate ID verification is a responsibility that must be taken seriously. Whether preventing underage sales, stopping identity fraud, or ensuring compliance with legal standards, businesses and institutions that handle identification documents must be vigilant in their processes. This involves a combination of proper training, access to the latest tools, and a deep understanding of the specific identification documents in circulation. With the increasing sophistication of fraudulent IDs and the critical role that identity plays in so many aspects of life, the need for accurate and precise verification has never been greater. Failure to implement robust ID verification measures not only jeopardizes the security and integrity of an organization but also exposes it to significant risks across legal, financial, and reputational fronts.

THE PURPOSE OF THIS GUIDE

The importance of accurately verifying identification in today's world cannot be overstated. With growing concerns over fraud, security threats, and legal compliance, the ability to correctly check and validate ID cards, particularly those issued by states, is becoming increasingly critical. This guide serves to bridge the knowledge gap that exists for those who handle ID verification daily—whether it's for businesses ensuring compliance with age restrictions, financial institutions combating identity fraud, or transportation agencies enforcing travel regulations. The overarching aim is to provide comprehensive information, insight, and strategies that make ID verification an exact science rather than a guessing game.

One of the primary purposes of this guide is to address the challenges associated with the variety of state-issued identification documents that exist in the United States. Each state has its own format, design, security features, and methods of issuing IDs, which can make the process of verification particularly complex. For those tasked with verifying IDs, it can be overwhelming to keep track of all the variations. This guide offers a detailed, state-by-state breakdown of identification cards, including driver's licenses and non-driver identification cards, to ensure that no matter where a person is from, their ID can be properly examined and authenticated. Having this level of detailed understanding helps to mitigate the risk of mistakes, particularly when an unfamiliar ID is presented.

Beyond the sheer variety of state IDs, it is also crucial to understand how these documents evolve over time. States frequently update their identification card designs, often incorporating new security features to combat the growing sophistication of counterfeit IDs. For example, many states now use holograms, UV images, or microprint text that is only visible under certain conditions. This guide serves the dual purpose of not only providing the current ID formats but also explaining how to interpret these security features, giving readers a deeper understanding of the mechanisms in place to prevent fraud. This is particularly important in industries like retail or hospitality, where employees may encounter customers from all over the country, each with IDs featuring different protective elements. By following the explanations provided here, users can make more informed decisions when examining an ID, knowing what to look for in terms of both standard information and advanced security features.

The guide also aims to clarify the legal obligations surrounding ID verification, which can be a significant source of confusion. Many people, especially those working in industries like alcohol retail, gambling, or transportation, may not fully understand the legal ramifications of failing to properly verify an ID. The laws governing ID verification vary not only by state but also by the specific circumstances under which the ID is being used. For instance, age verification for the sale of alcohol or tobacco is heavily regulated and comes with strict penalties for failure to comply, while other scenarios, such as checking IDs at hotels or rental agencies, may have different legal implications. This guide helps demystify these regulations, providing a clear explanation of both federal and state-level laws, ensuring that readers can approach ID verification with confidence. Knowing what is required by law can drastically reduce the risk of unintentional non-compliance, which can lead to severe penalties, including fines or loss of licenses.

In addition to helping readers understand their legal obligations, this guide emphasizes the importance of preventing fraud through accurate ID verification. Identity theft and counterfeit ID usage are on the rise, and criminals are becoming increasingly sophisticated in their methods. Fraudsters often target businesses or institutions where ID checks may not be as rigorous, taking advantage of loopholes or human error. For example, counterfeit IDs used in financial transactions can lead to significant monetary losses, as well as reputational damage for the business involved. The same is true in other sectors, such as hospitality or travel, where a failure to verify IDs properly could result in allowing individuals access to services or spaces that they are not entitled to, potentially leading to security breaches or legal liabilities. By learning to recognize the common signs of a fake or altered ID, such as mismatched fonts, incorrect placements of key information, or anomalies in the holographic elements, readers can become more adept at spotting fraudulent attempts. This guide provides extensive instruction on the common techniques used by counterfeiters, offering practical advice on how to identify them in real-world scenarios.

Another vital purpose of this guide is to ensure that ID verification processes are not only effective but also efficient. In high-volume environments like airports, casinos, or retail stores, time is often of the essence. Staff members need to be able to verify IDs quickly without compromising accuracy. The techniques outlined in this guide help streamline the verification process, teaching readers how to perform thorough checks in a time-effective manner. This includes not only manual inspection methods but also the use of modern technology such as ID scanners and mobile verification apps. These tools can rapidly identify many common types of ID fraud and ensure that key information, like date of birth or expiration date, is correctly captured and interpreted. As discussed in the earlier section on technological advances in ID verification, incorporating technology into the ID verification process can greatly enhance both the speed and accuracy of the checks being performed. Readers will find guidance on how to select and use these technologies effectively, balancing the need for speed with the importance of accuracy.

Ethical considerations also form a core part of this guide's purpose. When verifying an individual's identification, it is essential to ensure that the process is conducted fairly and without bias. Misidentifying or incorrectly rejecting a valid ID can lead to accusations of discrimination or unfair treatment, which can harm both the customer and the business. This guide provides best practices for handling ID verification in a way that is respectful, professional, and equitable. It encourages readers to treat all individuals equally, regardless of their appearance, background, or the state from which their ID was issued. By adhering to standardized procedures and being consistent in the application of verification protocols, those responsible for checking IDs can avoid common pitfalls, such as profiling or unfairly scrutinizing certain types of identification more than others. The goal is to maintain both security and customer service, ensuring that legitimate customers are treated fairly while fraudulent attempts are swiftly identified and dealt with.

Moreover, this guide aims to prepare readers for the future of ID verification. As the world becomes more digitized, identification methods are also evolving. The rise of mobile IDs and digital driver's licenses is already beginning to change the landscape of ID verification. Understanding how these new forms of ID function, what their security features are, and how to verify them properly is essential for staying ahead of future trends. This guide offers a forward-looking perspective on what to expect in the coming years, helping readers not only master the current processes but also prepare for upcoming changes. This includes an exploration of emerging technologies such as biometric verification, blockchain-based ID systems, and other innovations that promise to revolutionize how identity is authenticated in the digital age. As with traditional forms of ID, the key to effectively verifying these new types of identification will be understanding both their strengths and their vulnerabilities.

This guide serves as a comprehensive resource designed to equip readers with the knowledge, tools, and techniques necessary for accurate and efficient ID verification. Whether the goal is to comply with legal requirements, prevent fraud, enhance security, or provide better service to customers, the information contained here ensures that readers are fully prepared to handle the complexities of state-issued IDs in a modern, fast-paced world. With a deep understanding of the various formats, technologies, and laws involved in ID verification, readers can approach this critical task with confidence and competence, reducing the risks associated with improper verification and contributing to safer, more secure operations across all sectors.

CHAPTER 1

OVERVIEW OF ID VERIFICATION

LEGAL REQUIREMENTS FOR ID CHECKS

The legal requirements for ID checks in the United States are vast and vary significantly depending on the industry, the specific activity involved, and the laws of each state. At their core, ID checks serve two primary purposes: ensuring compliance with laws governing age-restricted products or activities, and verifying an individual's identity for security or financial reasons. Failing to adhere to the legal obligations surrounding ID verification can lead to serious consequences, including hefty fines, criminal charges, and in some cases, the loss of business licenses. Given the complexities of ID verification laws, it is crucial for businesses, institutions, and individuals responsible for checking identification to fully understand the scope of their legal responsibilities.

One of the most widely recognized legal obligations regarding ID checks relates to age verification. Federal and state laws strictly regulate the sale of age-restricted products such as alcohol, tobacco, and firearms. In most cases, retailers are required to verify the age of any customer who appears to be under a certain age—usually 21 for alcohol and 18 for tobacco, though state laws may vary. Failure to properly verify the age of a customer can result in fines, legal penalties, and in some cases, the revocation of a business's license to sell these products. While the requirement to check IDs in these instances might seem straightforward, the real challenge lies in the nuances of verifying the legitimacy of the ID presented. This is where a deep understanding of state-specific ID formats, security features, and the common methods of counterfeiting, as discussed in earlier sections, becomes essential.

In addition to verifying age for restricted products, ID checks are legally mandated in several other sectors, including financial services, air travel, and healthcare. Financial institutions, for instance, are bound by federal regulations to verify the identity of their customers as part of the "Know Your Customer" (KYC) requirements. These regulations, enforced by the U.S. Treasury's Financial Crimes Enforcement Network (FinCEN), are designed to prevent money laundering, terrorism financing, and other financial crimes. Under KYC laws, banks and other financial institutions must collect and verify identification information from customers before allowing them to open accounts or conduct large financial transactions. This includes not only verifying that the ID is genuine but also ensuring that the information provided matches the individual presenting it. This is particularly important in an age where identity theft and financial fraud are rampant. As noted in the section on the importance of accurate ID verification, failing to comply with KYC regulations can expose financial institutions to legal action, financial penalties, and reputational harm.

Airports and airlines are another area where legal requirements for ID checks are stringent. The Transportation Security Administration (TSA) mandates that all passengers must present valid identification before boarding a flight. This is primarily for security reasons, ensuring that individuals who pose a threat to public safety cannot easily pass through airport checkpoints. Additionally, the federal REAL ID Act, which sets minimum security standards for state-issued identification, has made compliance even more crucial. Starting in 2025, only REAL ID-compliant identification cards will be accepted for domestic air travel in the U.S., unless the individual presents a passport or other federally accepted form of identification. For airport staff and security personnel, understanding the differences between REAL ID-compliant and non-compliant IDs is now a legal necessity. This shift underscores the importance of staying informed about changes in ID laws and regulations, which will be a recurring theme as new technologies and legislative updates continue to shape the landscape of identification.

In the healthcare sector, ID checks are legally required in specific contexts, particularly when dealing with prescription medications or accessing certain types of medical care. Pharmacies, for instance, are required by law to verify the identity of individuals picking up controlled substances, such as opioid medications. This is part of an effort to combat the growing opioid crisis and prevent drug diversion. Proper ID verification ensures that prescriptions are dispensed only to the intended individual, reducing the risk of fraud or misuse. Similarly, hospitals and healthcare providers may be required to verify a patient's identity before administering treatments or performing procedures, particularly when the patient's insurance coverage is in question or when dealing with government-funded healthcare programs like Medicare and Medicaid. The legal obligation to accurately verify identities in these cases is not only a matter of compliance but also a critical factor in patient safety and fraud prevention. It reinforces the broader role that ID verification plays in protecting both individuals and institutions from harm.

Casinos and gambling establishments are yet another industry where legal requirements for ID checks are paramount. Both state and federal regulations require casinos to verify the identity and age of anyone engaging in gambling activities. This not only ensures that minors are not participating in gambling but also helps casinos comply with anti-money laundering regulations. The legal framework for casinos is stringent, requiring detailed record-keeping for any large cash transactions and the reporting of suspicious activities. Failure to properly verify IDs can lead to serious legal repercussions, including fines, loss of gaming licenses, and even criminal charges for facilitating illegal activities. Given the high volume of customers and large sums of money involved, casinos must strike a delicate balance between providing efficient service and meeting their legal obligations for ID verification. As with financial institutions, casinos are held to high standards when it comes to detecting fraudulent or altered IDs, making the guidance provided in earlier sections on spotting fake IDs and using ID scanners particularly relevant.

Another aspect of the legal requirements for ID checks revolves around privacy and data protection. While businesses and institutions are required to verify IDs in many cases, they must also handle the personal information collected during this process with care. Federal laws such as the Health Insurance Portability and Accountability Act (HIPAA) in healthcare and the Fair Credit Reporting Act (FCRA) in finance impose strict guidelines on how personal data should be stored, accessed, and used. These laws are designed to protect individuals' privacy and prevent unauthorized access to sensitive information. Mishandling the personal information collected during an ID check can lead to legal consequences, including lawsuits, fines, and reputational damage. For businesses that rely on ID verification as part of their operations, understanding these data protection laws is as important as knowing the legal requirements for the ID checks themselves. Proper training on both fronts can help reduce the risk of inadvertent violations.

While the federal government plays a significant role in establishing ID verification laws, individual states also have their own sets of regulations that govern ID checks. State laws may dictate who must verify IDs, under what circumstances, and the penalties for failing to do so. For example, some states have passed laws requiring businesses that sell alcohol or tobacco to implement ID scanning technology as part of their verification process. These scanners are intended to reduce human error and provide a more reliable method of confirming a person's age.

However, even in states where ID scanners are not legally required, businesses may choose to implement them voluntarily to ensure greater compliance with the law. As discussed in the section on technological advances in ID verification, the use of ID scanners and mobile apps can streamline the process, but it is important for businesses to remain aware of their legal obligations when using these tools, particularly regarding data retention and privacy concerns.

The legal requirements for ID checks extend beyond simply confirming someone's identity. They form part of a broader system of laws aimed at ensuring public safety, preventing fraud, and protecting privacy. Whether it's verifying the age of a customer, confirming the identity of a traveler, or preventing financial crime, the stakes for getting ID verification right are high. The consequences of failing to adhere to these legal obligations can be severe, ranging from financial penalties to loss of business licenses and even criminal charges. As such, it is essential for anyone involved in ID verification to have a thorough understanding of the legal landscape, both at the federal and state levels. Staying informed about changes in ID laws, understanding the specific requirements of their industry, and implementing best practices for ID verification are all key to meeting these legal obligations. By doing so, businesses and institutions not only protect themselves from legal and financial risks but also contribute to a safer and more secure environment for everyone involved.

COMMON SITUATIONS REQUIRING ID VERIFICATION

ID verification is a cornerstone of many everyday interactions across a wide range of industries. Whether it is ensuring compliance with legal regulations, safeguarding security, or preventing fraud, ID checks are embedded in numerous processes where identity validation is critical. The need for verification spans a spectrum of scenarios, from purchasing age-restricted products to boarding a plane, each presenting unique challenges and requirements. Understanding the various situations that commonly require ID verification is essential not only for legal compliance but also for ensuring that these checks are conducted accurately and efficiently, as previously discussed in sections dealing with the legal requirements and the importance of proper ID verification.

One of the most frequent situations requiring ID verification involves the sale of age-restricted products such as alcohol, tobacco, and lottery tickets. Retailers, bars, restaurants, and other establishments that sell these products are legally obligated to verify the age of customers to ensure compliance with federal, state, and local laws. For instance, alcohol can only be sold to individuals over the age of 21 in the United States, while tobacco sales are restricted to those over the age of 18 or 21, depending on the state. Failure to conduct proper age verification not only results in significant legal penalties but also risks contributing to underage consumption. This makes accurate ID verification paramount in these settings, as discussed earlier in the context of legal obligations. Cashiers, bartenders, and other employees are often the first line of defense in ensuring that minors do not gain access to restricted products, and their ability to distinguish between valid and fraudulent IDs is crucial. In these situations, having a detailed understanding of the nuances of state-issued IDs, as explored in previous sections, is vital for spotting any irregularities that may signal a counterfeit or altered document.

ID verification is also a key requirement in financial institutions, particularly when it comes to opening bank accounts, applying for loans, or conducting large transactions. The banking industry is heavily regulated, and institutions are required to comply with federal laws such as the "Know Your Customer" (KYC) regulations. These rules are designed to prevent money laundering, terrorism financing, and other illicit financial activities. When a new customer opens an account, the bank must verify their identity by checking government-issued identification, such as a driver's license or passport, to confirm that the person is who they claim to be. Similarly, during large transactions or changes to an account, ID checks are necessary to protect against fraud and ensure that the correct person is accessing the funds. The detailed guidelines for verifying IDs in these contexts are integral not only for compliance but also for protecting both the institution and the customer from financial harm, as noted in earlier sections of the role ID verification plays in fraud prevention.

Airports and other transportation hubs present another common scenario where ID verification is mandatory. For air travel, the Transportation Security Administration (TSA) requires all passengers to present valid identification before boarding a flight. This security measure is designed to prevent individuals who may pose a threat from boarding planes and to ensure that passengers are correctly identified before travel. In addition to government-issued IDs such as driver's licenses and passports, passengers may also present other forms of identification that meet the TSA's criteria. The REAL ID Act, which establishes stricter security standards for state-issued IDs, has further increased the importance of proper ID verification in air travel. Beginning in 2025, only REAL ID-compliant identification will be accepted for domestic air travel in the United States, unless the traveler presents an alternative form of federal identification. As discussed previously, understanding the distinction between REAL ID-compliant and non-compliant forms of identification is crucial for airport staff, security personnel, and travelers alike. Mistakes in this process can lead to significant delays, missed flights, and security risks, making accuracy in ID checks an essential part of the travel experience.

Another critical area where ID verification plays a pivotal role is in the healthcare industry. Hospitals, clinics, and pharmacies frequently check IDs to verify the identity of patients and to ensure that medical records are accurately linked to the correct individual. This is especially important when dealing with sensitive health information or when dispensing prescription medications, particularly controlled substances. As noted earlier in the section on legal requirements, healthcare providers are required to verify the identity of patients picking up prescriptions for controlled substances to prevent drug diversion and misuse. Failure to properly check IDs in these settings can result in serious consequences, both in terms of patient safety and legal liability for the institution. The healthcare sector's reliance on accurate ID verification also extends to situations where individuals are accessing insurance benefits or government-funded healthcare programs like Medicare and Medicaid, where identity fraud can have significant financial implications.

Casinos and gambling establishments provide another example of situations where ID checks are not only common but also legally mandated. Federal and state regulations require casinos to verify the age and identity of anyone who participates in gambling activities. This is partly to ensure that minors are not allowed to gamble and partly to comply with anti-money laundering laws. Casinos are also required to keep detailed records of high-value transactions and report suspicious activity, all of which necessitate thorough ID verification. The large sums of money that change hands in casinos make them attractive targets for fraud and criminal activity, underscoring the importance of rigorous ID checks. As previously mentioned in the context of financial institutions, the accuracy and speed with which ID checks are performed can be critical in these high-stakes environments. In casinos, employees must be trained to quickly assess the legitimacy of IDs, including recognizing the various security features of state-issued documents, as discussed in the earlier section on understanding ID formats.

The rental car industry and hotels are two additional sectors where ID verification is routinely required. When renting a car, the rental agency needs to confirm the identity of the renter and ensure that they have a valid driver's license. This verification process is necessary for both legal and insurance purposes, as renting a vehicle to someone without a valid license could expose the company to liability in the event of an accident. Similarly, hotels often require guests to present identification when checking in. This serves multiple purposes, including verifying that the person making the reservation is indeed the individual checking into the room, as well as ensuring that the guest is of legal age to book a room. In both cases, accurate ID verification protects the business from fraud and liability while ensuring compliance with any applicable regulations.

In addition to these commonly encountered situations, there are numerous other contexts where ID verification is necessary. For instance, many employers require new hires to provide identification when completing the I-9 form, which verifies the employee's legal eligibility to work in the United States. In this scenario, the employer is legally obligated to inspect the employee's identification documents to ensure that they are authentic and belong to the person being hired. Similarly, ID verification is often required in educational settings, particularly when students are taking standardized tests or applying for financial aid. Schools and testing centers must verify the identity of students to ensure that the correct individual is present and to prevent cheating or fraud.

The need for ID verification is also prominent in government services, such as when individuals apply for social security benefits, driver's licenses, or passports. In each of these instances, government agencies are responsible for verifying the applicant's identity to ensure that the benefits or documents are issued to the correct individual. Failure to properly verify identities in these situations can lead to identity theft, fraud, and other serious legal and financial consequences.

The situations that require ID verification are numerous and varied, spanning a broad spectrum of industries and activities. Whether it's verifying the age of a customer purchasing alcohol, confirming a passenger's identity at an airport, or checking the credentials of a new employee, accurate and efficient ID verification is a critical part of ensuring compliance, security, and fraud prevention. As discussed throughout this book, understanding the nuances of ID verification—from recognizing the security features of state-issued IDs to staying informed about legal requirements—empowers businesses and institutions to meet their responsibilities with confidence. Each of these common scenarios underscores the importance of proper training and awareness in ID verification, ensuring that those responsible for conducting these checks are equipped with the knowledge and tools they need to perform this vital task effectively.

CONSEQUENCES OF IMPROPER ID VERIFICATION

The consequences of improper ID verification can be far-reaching, affecting not only businesses and institutions but also individuals and society at large. While the importance of accurate ID verification has been discussed in earlier sections, particularly in relation to the legal and practical requirements that govern various industries, it is critical to understand the severe repercussions that can arise from lapses or failures in this process. Improper ID verification can lead to a host of issues, ranging from legal penalties and financial losses to threats to public safety and reputational damage. The cascading effects of inadequate checks underscore why meticulous attention to detail and a clear understanding of ID verification protocols are essential for anyone tasked with this responsibility.

One of the most immediate and serious consequences of improper ID verification is legal liability. Businesses, institutions, and individuals who are required by law to verify identities must do so with care, as failing to comply with legal mandates can result in severe penalties. This is particularly true for age-restricted products like alcohol, tobacco, and firearms, where improper verification can lead to sales to minors or unauthorized individuals. In such cases, businesses may face fines, legal actions, and even the revocation of their licenses to operate. For example, a liquor store that fails to properly verify the age of a customer who purchases alcohol could be held legally accountable if the individual is later found to be underage. Similarly, selling tobacco or firearms to an individual without conducting thorough ID checks can lead to significant legal consequences. The importance of maintaining strict compliance with age-verification laws, as discussed earlier, cannot be overstated. These legal requirements are designed to protect public health and safety, and failing to adhere to them can have lasting negative impacts on both the business and the community it serves.

In the financial sector, improper ID verification can expose institutions to the risk of fraud, money laundering, and identity theft. Banks, credit unions, and other financial institutions are required to comply with regulations such as the "Know Your Customer" (KYC) guidelines, which mandate that they verify the identity of their customers before allowing them to open accounts or conduct significant financial transactions. If these institutions fail to properly verify a customer's ID, they risk enabling fraudulent activities, including the use of fake identities to open accounts or launder money. Such failures can lead to regulatory fines, legal action, and significant reputational damage. The regulatory landscape for financial institutions is strict, and non-compliance with KYC laws can result in millions of dollars in fines, as well as loss of customer trust. In a sector where trust and security are paramount, improper ID verification can be particularly devastating, not only resulting in financial losses but also damaging the institution's long-term viability and reputation.

Beyond the financial implications, improper ID verification can also pose serious security risks. In environments like airports, government buildings, and other high-security areas, failure to accurately verify the identity of individuals can lead to security breaches with potentially catastrophic consequences. As previously discussed in the section on common situations requiring ID verification, the Transportation Security Administration (TSA) requires travelers to present valid identification before boarding flights to ensure that no unauthorized individuals gain access to restricted areas. If airport personnel fail to properly verify IDs, the risk of allowing dangerous individuals to board flights or enter secure areas increases significantly. Such lapses in security could have far-reaching consequences, potentially endangering the lives of passengers and crew members. In these high-stakes environments, even a small mistake in ID verification can lead to devastating outcomes. The introduction of the REAL ID Act, as noted earlier, has further heightened the importance of ensuring that ID checks are conducted correctly, as only REAL ID-compliant documents will be accepted for domestic air travel starting in 2025. Failing to adhere to these standards could compromise national security and lead to significant operational disruptions.

In addition to security concerns, improper ID verification can also have severe implications for public health and safety. In the healthcare sector, for example, verifying the identity of patients is crucial for ensuring that medical records are accurate and that treatments are administered to the correct individual. If a healthcare provider fails to properly verify a patient's identity, it could lead to medical errors, such as administering the wrong medication or procedure. In some cases, these errors can have life-threatening consequences. Furthermore, pharmacies are required to verify the identity of individuals picking up controlled substances to prevent drug diversion and misuse. Improper ID verification in this context can contribute to the opioid crisis and other public health issues by allowing drugs to fall into the wrong hands. As noted in previous sections about legal requirements for ID checks in healthcare, accurate verification processes are essential for protecting both patients and the broader community from harm.

Improper ID verification can also have profound consequences for businesses and institutions in terms of reputational damage. In today's highly connected world, news of a business's failure to properly verify IDs can spread quickly, particularly if the lapse results in significant harm or legal action. For instance, a nightclub that is found to have allowed minors to enter without proper ID checks may face public outrage, legal action, and potential boycotts from customers. Similarly, financial institutions that fail to prevent identity theft or fraud due to inadequate ID verification protocols can lose the trust of their customers, which can take years to rebuild. As previously discussed in the context of fraud prevention, businesses must be vigilant in their ID verification processes to avoid these types of reputational risks. Trust is a key component of the relationship between businesses and their customers, and any perceived weakness in a business's ability to protect its customers from harm can result in long-lasting damage.

Another critical consequence of improper ID verification is the potential for identity theft and fraud. When businesses or institutions fail to properly verify the identities of individuals, they open the door to criminals who use fake or stolen IDs to commit fraud. Identity theft can result in significant financial losses for both the victims and the businesses involved. For instance, if a criminal uses a stolen ID to open a bank account or apply for a credit card, the financial institution may be held responsible for any losses incurred by the victim. The costs of rectifying identity theft can be enormous, both in terms of financial compensation and the time and resources required to restore the victim's credit and identity. In some cases, victims of identity theft may suffer long-term financial and emotional damage, as their credit scores, savings, and personal security are compromised. This underscores the importance of proper training and protocols for those responsible for verifying IDs, as discussed in earlier sections. Ensuring that employees are well-versed in the methods of detecting fraudulent IDs is essential for minimizing the risk of identity theft and fraud.

Improper ID verification can also lead to administrative inefficiencies and operational disruptions. When businesses or institutions fail to verify IDs correctly, it can lead to errors in record-keeping, misidentification, and the need for time-consuming corrections. In some cases, these errors can disrupt operations and cause significant delays. For example, a bank that mistakenly approves an account for an individual using a fake ID may have to go through a lengthy process to close the account, investigate the fraud, and rectify any resulting financial discrepancies. Similarly, airports that fail to properly verify traveler IDs may face delays in processing passengers, leading to longer wait times, missed flights, and customer dissatisfaction. These operational disruptions not only affect the efficiency of the business but also its bottom line, as customers who experience delays or errors may be less likely to return in the future. The importance of efficient and accurate ID verification, as previously discussed, cannot be overstated in these high-volume environments where the margin for error is small.

The consequences of improper ID verification are broad and varied, affecting legal compliance, financial stability, security, public safety, and reputational integrity. As discussed throughout this book, the importance of accurate and efficient ID verification cannot be overstated, as the risks associated with improper checks can have far-reaching implications. Whether it's a retail store selling age-restricted products, a financial institution conducting KYC checks, or an airport verifying passenger IDs, the stakes are high. Those responsible for conducting ID checks must be properly trained and equipped to carry out their duties with precision and care, as even small lapses can result in significant harm. The integration of technology, the understanding of legal frameworks, and the ability to recognize fraudulent documents are all essential components of an effective ID verification process, as explored in earlier sections. Ultimately, the consequences of improper ID verification highlight the critical role that these checks play in maintaining the safety, security, and trust that are foundational to both individual and societal well-being.

CHAPTER 2

UNDERSTANDING DIFFERENT ID TYPES

GOVERNMENT-ISSUED IDS

Government-issued IDs form the backbone of identity verification systems across the United States. These documents, issued by federal, state, and local authorities, serve as official proof of identity and are essential in a wide array of situations, ranging from everyday transactions to high-security environments. The significance of these IDs lies not only in their legal authority but also in the level of security and trust associated with them. For any individual or entity tasked with verifying identity, understanding the nuances of government-issued IDs is critical to ensuring compliance with regulations, safeguarding against fraud, and maintaining the integrity of various processes that require identity authentication. Building on previous sections about the importance of accurate ID verification and the legal requirements surrounding it, this section delves deeper into the complexities of government-issued IDs, examining their formats, features, and their role in ensuring public trust and security.

One of the most commonly used forms of government-issued ID in the United States is the driver's license, issued by each state's Department of Motor Vehicles (DMV). A driver's license not only serves as proof of the individual's ability to operate a motor vehicle but also functions as a widely accepted form of identification for numerous purposes. Whether used for opening a bank account, purchasing age-restricted products, or boarding a domestic flight, the driver's license is perhaps the most frequently presented form of ID. The wide acceptance of driver's licenses stems from their standardized issuance process and the inclusion of multiple security features designed to prevent tampering and counterfeiting. As mentioned in earlier sections, understanding these features is crucial for anyone responsible for verifying IDs. Driver's licenses typically include holograms, barcodes, magnetic strips, and other visual and digital elements that ensure their authenticity. Verifying these features is a key component in ensuring that the ID being presented is both legitimate and unaltered.

The implementation of the REAL ID Act has further increased the significance of state-issued driver's licenses. The REAL ID Act, passed in 2005, sets federal standards for the issuance of IDs, particularly for their use in accessing federal facilities and boarding commercial aircraft. Beginning in 2025, only REAL ID-compliant licenses or other federally accepted forms of identification will be permitted for domestic air travel. This shift highlights the growing importance of standardization and security in government-issued IDs. The distinction between a REAL ID-compliant license and a standard one lies in the additional security features and documentation required for issuance. To obtain a REAL ID, applicants must provide proof of identity, such as a birth certificate or passport, proof of residency, and proof of their Social Security number, among other documentation. This process ensures that the individual's identity is thoroughly vetted before a REAL ID-compliant document is issued. As we discussed earlier in relation to legal requirements, the transition to REAL ID standards has necessitated changes in how IDs are verified, particularly in settings such as airports and federal buildings where security is paramount.

In addition to driver's licenses, another common form of government-issued ID is the U.S. passport. A passport serves as both a travel document and a universally accepted form of identification within and outside the country. Issued by the U.S. Department of State, passports contain a wide range of security features that make them difficult to forge or alter. These features include watermarks, microprinting, ultraviolet light elements, and embedded chips that store biometric data, such as the passport holder's fingerprints or photograph. Passports are especially important in contexts where individuals need to prove their citizenship, such as when applying for government benefits, registering to vote, or traveling internationally. The passport's robust security features make it a trusted form of identification for high-security purposes, such as gaining entry to federal buildings or boarding international flights. As mentioned previously in relation to security risks, the accuracy and thoroughness of ID verification play a crucial role in ensuring that only legitimate passport holders gain access to restricted areas or privileges.

For individuals who do not drive or hold a passport, state identification cards offer an alternative form of government-issued ID. These non-driver ID cards are typically issued by state DMVs and are often similar in appearance to driver's licenses, though they do not grant driving privileges. Like driver's licenses, state ID cards include security features designed to prevent counterfeiting and tampering, making them a reliable form of identification in situations where proof of identity or age is required. For instance, state ID cards are frequently used by elderly individuals, non-drivers, and minors who need to verify their identity for age-restricted purchases, healthcare services, or access to certain facilities. These IDs are critical for ensuring that individuals who do not hold a driver's license still have access to a recognized form of identification. As discussed in the section on legal requirements for ID verification, state-issued IDs must meet certain standards of authenticity, and those responsible for verifying them should be well-versed in recognizing the security features that distinguish legitimate documents from forgeries.

Government-issued IDs are also critical in the context of employment. The U.S. Citizenship and Immigration Services (USCIS) requires employers to verify the identity and employment eligibility of new hires through the I-9 form process. Employees must present acceptable forms of identification, such as a Social Security card, passport, or driver's license, alongside documents proving their right to work in the U.S. For employers, properly verifying these documents is a legal obligation that helps prevent unauthorized employment and ensures compliance with federal regulations. Failing to accurately verify an employee's identity can result in significant legal penalties for the employer, as well as potential disruptions to business operations. As discussed earlier, the consequences of improper ID verification are far-reaching, particularly when it comes to legal compliance in high-stakes environments like employment.

Another widely used government-issued ID is the Social Security card, issued by the Social Security Administration. Although it is not typically used as a standalone form of photo ID, the Social Security card plays a crucial role in verifying an individual's identity, particularly in employment, tax, and benefit-related contexts. The Social Security number (SSN) printed on the card is a unique identifier that is used in a variety of legal and financial transactions, including applying for credit, filing taxes, and receiving government benefits such as Social Security or Medicare. Because of its importance, the Social Security card is frequently targeted by identity thieves, making it essential for institutions to verify its authenticity when used as part of an identity verification process. The potential for identity theft, as discussed in earlier sections, highlights the importance of careful and thorough ID checks when handling sensitive documents like Social Security cards.

Other forms of government-issued IDs, such as military identification cards, green cards (permanent resident cards), and tribal identification cards, also play significant roles in identity verification. Military IDs, for instance, are used by active-duty service members, veterans, and their dependents to access military facilities, healthcare services, and other benefits. These IDs include advanced security features such as embedded chips and holographic elements to prevent forgery. Green cards, issued by USCIS, serve as proof of lawful permanent residency in the United States and are critical for non-citizens seeking employment, travel, or access to certain government services. Tribal identification cards, issued by federally recognized Native American tribes, are used for similar purposes and are recognized as valid forms of identification under federal law.

Given the variety of government-issued IDs in circulation, those tasked with verifying identities must have a comprehensive understanding of the different types of documents, their features, and the legal requirements for their use. As discussed in earlier sections on the consequences of improper ID verification, failing to accurately verify government-issued IDs can lead to serious legal, financial, and security risks. Whether in the context of preventing underage sales, complying with employment regulations, or safeguarding national security, the role of government-issued IDs is central to the integrity of identity verification processes across the country.

Government-issued IDs serve as the foundation for identity verification in the United States, providing a trusted and secure means of confirming an individual's identity across a wide range of contexts. From driver's licenses and passports to Social Security cards and military IDs, these documents are designed with robust security features that help protect against fraud and ensure the legitimacy of the identification process. As explored throughout this book, the accuracy and diligence with which these IDs are verified play a critical role in maintaining the trust and security that underpin society's most essential systems. Understanding the various forms of government-issued IDs, as well as the legal and practical implications of verifying them, is crucial for ensuring compliance, preventing fraud, and protecting public safety.

DRIVER'S LICENSES VS. NON-DRIVER IDS

The distinction between driver's licenses and non-driver IDs is one that carries significant importance in the realm of identity verification. While both documents serve as government-issued identification, they fulfill different purposes and cater to distinct segments of the population. Understanding the differences between these forms of identification is essential for anyone involved in verifying identities, as both documents play a key role in confirming a person's identity in various legal, financial, and commercial settings. Despite their similarities in appearance and the fact that they are issued by state authorities, the contexts in which these IDs are used, and the legal responsibilities associated with them, vary considerably. This section will explore these distinctions in detail, referencing relevant points covered in previous sections regarding government-issued IDs and the legal framework surrounding them, ensuring a comprehensive understanding of the nuances between these two critical forms of identification.

A driver's license is, first and foremost, a document that grants an individual the legal authority to operate a motor vehicle. Issued by the Department of Motor Vehicles (DMV) or equivalent state agencies, the primary function of a driver's license is to certify that the individual has passed the required tests and is qualified to drive. However, driver's licenses also serve as one of the most widely accepted forms of government-issued identification in the United States. Their dual functionality makes them one of the most commonly presented IDs in situations ranging from routine transactions, such as opening a bank account or purchasing age-restricted products, to more critical scenarios, such as verifying identity for voting or air travel. As discussed in the section on government-issued IDs, the driver's license is often the default form of identification for most Americans, given its ubiquitous nature and the fact that many adults need it for practical reasons related to transportation.

In addition to verifying the ability to drive, driver's licenses contain essential identity-related information, including the individual's full name, date of birth, address, photograph, and, in most cases, a unique identifying number. Over time, states have enhanced the security features of driver's licenses to protect against fraud, including the addition of holograms, barcodes, magnetic strips, and, increasingly, biometric data embedded in the document. These features are crucial in the context of ID verification, as they provide a means for businesses and institutions to ensure that the document is genuine and has not been tampered with. The security of driver's licenses has become even more important in recent years with the introduction of the REAL ID Act, which sets federal standards for the issuance of state-issued IDs. As previously noted in our section of the REAL ID Act, driver's licenses that comply with these federal standards will be required for domestic air travel and access to certain federal facilities starting in 2025. This underscores the growing importance of the driver's license as a trusted form of identification not only at the state level but also at the federal level.

Non-driver IDs, on the other hand, are issued primarily for the purpose of identification rather than for driving. These IDs are designed for individuals who do not drive or do not need a license but still require a valid government-issued document to prove their identity. Like driver's licenses, non-driver IDs are issued by state DMVs or other state agencies, and they typically include the same core information, such as the individual's name, date of birth, photograph, and address. Non-driver IDs also feature many of the same security elements as driver's licenses, including holographic overlays, barcodes, and other anti-counterfeiting measures, making them just as secure and reliable as driver's licenses in terms of verifying identity. These security measures are crucial for ensuring that non-driver IDs cannot be easily forged or altered, a point that was emphasized earlier in our broader section of the importance of secure ID verification to prevent fraud and identity theft.

The primary distinction between these two forms of ID lies in their purpose. While a driver's license authorizes the individual to operate a vehicle and also serves as a form of identification, a non-driver ID is purely an identity document. This makes non-driver IDs particularly valuable for individuals who do not drive due to age, disability, or personal preference. For example, elderly individuals who no longer drive but still need a valid ID for banking, healthcare, and other purposes can obtain a non-driver ID to meet their identification needs. Similarly, minors who are not yet of legal driving age but require an ID for travel, school, or employment may use a non-driver ID. As we discussed earlier in the section on common situations requiring ID verification, there are many scenarios where proof of identity is essential, and non-driver IDs serve as a crucial alternative for those who do not possess a driver's license.

One area where the differences between driver's licenses and non-driver IDs become especially relevant is in the verification process. For those tasked with verifying IDs, understanding the subtle distinctions between these two documents is important. While both types of ID contain the necessary elements to confirm a person's identity, the absence of driving-related endorsements or restrictions on a non-driver ID means that its sole function is to verify identity. This can simplify the verification process in contexts where the ability to drive is irrelevant, such as verifying age for purchasing alcohol or tobacco, or confirming identity for voting. As noted earlier in our section of legal requirements for ID checks, different states have varying rules for what forms of ID are acceptable in certain contexts, and understanding the difference between a driver's license and a non-driver ID can help ensure that the correct type of ID is presented in each situation.

The rise of non-driver IDs has also been driven by the growing demand for accessible forms of identification that cater to diverse populations. In many states, individuals who do not drive may face significant barriers when trying to access services that require ID, particularly in rural areas where public transportation options are limited. Non-driver IDs offer a solution to this problem, providing individuals with a secure and reliable form of identification without the need to obtain a driver's license. This has become particularly important in the context of voting, as many states have implemented voter ID laws that require individuals to present a valid government-issued ID at the polls. For individuals who do not drive, a non-driver ID is often the most practical and accessible option. As discussed in earlier sections, the legal requirements for ID verification in certain contexts, such as voting, can have significant implications for accessibility and participation, making non-driver IDs a critical tool for ensuring that all individuals have the ability to meet these requirements.

Another key consideration when comparing driver's licenses and non-driver IDs is the process of obtaining these documents. While both types of ID are issued by state authorities, the requirements for obtaining a driver's license are typically more stringent, as individuals must pass both written and practical driving tests to demonstrate their ability to operate a vehicle. In contrast, obtaining a non-driver ID generally requires only proof of identity, residency, and, in some cases, legal presence in the United States. This makes the non-driver ID a more accessible option for individuals who do not need to prove their ability to drive but still require a valid form of identification. As discussed earlier in the section on legal requirements for ID checks, the documentation required for obtaining government-issued IDs is an important factor in ensuring that these documents can be trusted and relied upon for accurate identity verification.

Both driver's licenses and non-driver IDs play essential roles in the landscape of identity verification in the United States. While a driver's license serves the dual purpose of granting driving privileges and providing a trusted form of identification, non-driver IDs are designed specifically for individuals who do not drive but still need a valid and secure form of ID. The similarities between these two types of ID, particularly in terms of their security features and the information they contain, make them equally reliable for confirming identity in various legal, financial, and commercial contexts. However, the differences in their issuance, purpose, and use are important to understand for anyone tasked with verifying IDs, as these distinctions can impact the verification process depending on the situation. As explored in previous sections, the accuracy and thoroughness of ID verification are critical for maintaining legal compliance, preventing fraud, and protecting public safety, and understanding the nuances between driver's licenses and non-driver IDs is a key part of this broader effort.

PASSPORTS AND PASSPORT CARDS

Passports and passport cards are essential forms of government-issued identification that play a critical role in both domestic and international contexts. While passports are primarily used for international travel, they also serve as highly secure proof of identity in various situations where a high level of verification is required. Passport cards, on the other hand, offer a more convenient option for travel within specific geographic areas while also serving as a legitimate form of identification within the United States. Both documents are issued by the U.S. Department of State and contain advanced security features that make them reliable and difficult to forge. As we explore the nuances of these two important forms of identification, it is essential to consider the broader implications of their use in ID verification processes, building on previous sections around government-issued IDs and the consequences of improper verification.

A U.S. passport is an internationally recognized travel document that certifies the identity and nationality of its holder. It allows the bearer to travel to foreign countries and serves as proof of their legal right to re-enter the United States. Passports contain several critical pieces of information, including the holder's full name, photograph, date of birth, place of birth, and the dates of issue and expiration. Additionally, modern U.S. passports are equipped with an embedded electronic chip that stores the holder's biometric data, such as their facial image or fingerprints, which adds an additional layer of security. The biometric data ensures that the document is tied to the individual in a way that is difficult to counterfeit, enhancing the reliability of the passport as a trusted form of identification. This is particularly important in contexts where high-security identification is required, such as when entering federal buildings or boarding international flights. As noted in our earlier section on government-issued IDs, the security features embedded in these documents are a crucial factor in preventing fraud and maintaining the integrity of the verification process.

In addition to serving as a travel document, the U.S. passport is also accepted as a valid form of identification in numerous non-travel-related situations. For example, it can be used to verify identity when opening a bank account, applying for a mortgage, or even voting in states where a government-issued ID is required. Because the passport is issued by the federal government and contains advanced security features, it is considered one of the most secure forms of identification available. The inclusion of biometric data in passports, which is scanned during the issuance process, ensures that the identity of the individual is thoroughly vetted and protected against fraudulent use. This makes the passport a highly trusted form of identification in environments where the accuracy and legitimacy of the document must be beyond doubt, especially in high-stakes scenarios like border crossings or when accessing sensitive government services.

In contrast, the U.S. passport card is a more compact version of the traditional passport, designed for limited travel and identification purposes. While it contains the same basic information as a full passport—such as the holder's name, photograph, and citizenship status—the passport card is smaller in size and lacks some of the biometric features found in the full passport. The passport card can be used for travel by land and sea to neighboring countries such as Canada, Mexico, and certain Caribbean nations, but it is not valid for international air travel. However, like the passport, the card is also a government-issued ID that meets high standards of security and verification. The U.S. Department of State issues passport cards with several anti-fraud measures, including microprinting, secure lamination, and ultraviolet images, which make them difficult to counterfeit. This ensures that even though the passport card is more limited in its travel applications, it remains a reliable form of identification.

The key difference between a passport and a passport card lies in their intended use. Passports are designed for global travel and are accepted in nearly every country as a form of identification and proof of nationality. In contrast, passport cards are intended for more localized travel within North America and the Caribbean. However, despite these differences in scope, both the passport and passport card carry equal weight when used within the United States for identity verification purposes. A passport card may not be used to fly internationally, but it is still considered a valid ID for domestic air travel, voting, or any other situation where a government-issued ID is required. This versatility makes passport cards an appealing option for individuals who do not anticipate needing a full passport but still want a federally issued, secure form of identification for everyday use.

It is important to consider how passports and passport cards fit into the broader landscape of identity verification in the U.S. In previous sections, we touched on the importance of secure identification in high-risk environments, such as employment verification or access to age-restricted services. Passports, given their federal issuance and stringent verification process, offer a high level of security and trust in these scenarios. For example, employers may accept a U.S. passport or passport card as proof of both identity and work authorization during the I-9 verification process. This use of passports in employment verification highlights how critical it is to accurately assess the authenticity of these documents, as improper verification can result in legal liabilities for employers and potentially serious consequences for the employee. As explored earlier, the risks of improper ID verification extend beyond legal consequences, including the possibility of enabling fraud, identity theft, or unauthorized access to sensitive services.

Another relevant aspect to consider is the process of obtaining these documents. Obtaining a U.S. passport or passport card requires an individual to provide extensive proof of their identity, citizenship, and residency. Typically, this involves presenting a combination of documents, such as a birth certificate, driver's license, and Social Security card, to establish the individual's identity. Once this documentation has been reviewed and verified, the passport is issued, usually within several weeks. This thorough vetting process is one of the reasons why passports are so highly regarded as secure forms of identification. Because the application process involves multiple layers of verification, it is more difficult for individuals to fraudulently obtain a passport compared to other forms of ID. As we discussed in earlier sections, the accuracy and legitimacy of the documents presented during the application process are paramount in ensuring the overall integrity of identity verification systems.

In terms of the design and security features of these documents, U.S. passports are among the most advanced government-issued IDs available. The passport's embedded electronic chip, which stores the individual's biometric information, is part of the global trend towards more secure, tamper-proof identification systems. The chip can be read by electronic scanners at airports and border checkpoints, making it nearly impossible for someone to alter the document without detection. This biometric layer adds an extra level of security, as it allows for real-time comparison of the data stored on the chip with the individual presenting the passport. In contrast, while passport cards contain numerous physical security features, such as holograms and microprinting, they do not include biometric data or electronic chips. This makes them somewhat less secure for high-stakes verification, but their compact size and convenience make them an appealing option for travelers who do not need the full capabilities of a traditional passport.

Both U.S. passports and passport cards are crucial tools for identity verification, each with its own specific advantages and limitations. Passports offer the highest level of security and are accepted internationally, making them essential for global travel and for use in situations where the individual's identity must be verified beyond doubt. Passport cards, while more limited in their travel applications, still provide a highly secure and reliable form of identification for domestic use and travel to certain neighboring countries. Both documents, issued by the U.S. Department of State, are equipped with advanced security features that make them resistant to tampering and forgery, ensuring that they can be trusted for accurate and reliable identity verification. As explored throughout this book, the process of verifying these documents requires attention to detail and an understanding of the security features that distinguish legitimate documents from forgeries. By understanding the differences between passports and passport cards, individuals and organizations can make informed decisions about which form of identification is best suited for their specific needs, while ensuring compliance with legal standards and safeguarding against fraud.

MILITARY IDS AND TRIBAL IDS

Military IDs and Tribal IDs serve as two unique, yet critically important, forms of identification within the broader landscape of U.S. government-issued IDs. While both types of ID fulfill specific functions and cater to distinct communities, they share a common purpose: verifying the identity and status of individuals in various situations. Military IDs are primarily issued to members of the U.S. Armed Forces, their dependents, and military retirees, serving both as proof of military service and as a means of accessing military benefits and privileges. Tribal IDs, on the other hand, are issued by Native American tribes to their members, establishing both tribal membership and serving as a form of legal identification. Each type of ID carries distinct features, legal requirements, and verification processes that make them integral to identity verification procedures in different contexts.

Military IDs are issued by the Department of Defense (DoD) and are used to identify active-duty service members, reservists, National Guard members, retirees, and their dependents. The primary function of a military ID is to confirm an individual's affiliation with the U.S. Armed Forces, but it also serves as a highly secure form of government-issued identification. Military IDs are equipped with numerous security features to prevent forgery and unauthorized use, including barcodes, magnetic strips, and, in some cases, embedded microchips that store encrypted information about the cardholder. These security measures ensure that the ID is not only a trusted document for accessing military installations and services but also serves as a reliable form of identification outside of military contexts, such as when opening bank accounts, verifying identity in legal proceedings, or accessing other government services.

One of the most distinctive aspects of military IDs is their incorporation of personal data that is tied specifically to the individual's role within the military. Active-duty personnel, for instance, have IDs that contain information about their rank, branch of service, and expiration dates that coincide with their enlistment term. Retired military personnel hold different types of IDs, often referred to as retiree IDs, which confirm their retired status and allow them to continue accessing certain military benefits, such as healthcare and commissary privileges. Dependents of military personnel also receive their own form of military identification, commonly known as the Uniformed Services ID Card, which allows them to access certain services and benefits related to their sponsor's military service. This structured system of identification ensures that military personnel and their families are properly recognized and authorized to access benefits, while also providing a reliable way for civilian institutions to verify military affiliation.

Tribal IDs, on the other hand, are issued by federally recognized Native American tribes and play a crucial role in establishing an individual's membership within a specific tribe. While the issuance of Tribal IDs is governed by the tribe itself, these IDs are legally recognized by the U.S. federal government and state governments as valid forms of identification in many contexts. Tribal IDs are essential for Native American individuals in affirming their identity and citizenship within their respective tribes, and they are often required for accessing certain federal programs, such as health services provided through the Indian Health Service (IHS), and for asserting rights tied to tribal land and resources. The design and features of Tribal IDs can vary significantly between tribes, but they generally include important details such as the individual's name, photograph, tribal affiliation, enrollment number, and date of birth.

Like military IDs, Tribal IDs are designed to be secure and difficult to forge, often incorporating similar security features such as holograms, barcodes, and unique serial numbers. However, one challenge that arises in verifying Tribal IDs is the variation in design and issuance standards among different tribes. Because each tribe has the authority to design and issue its own IDs, there is no universal template for what a Tribal ID looks like, unlike military IDs, which follow a standardized format set by the Department of Defense. This lack of uniformity can make it more difficult for institutions unfamiliar with Tribal IDs to verify their authenticity. Nevertheless, Tribal IDs are still legally recognized in many contexts, including voting, enrolling in federal assistance programs, and proving eligibility for certain treaty rights and privileges reserved for Native American communities. The importance of accurate verification of these documents cannot be understated, as improper verification could deny individuals access to services and rights to which they are legally entitled.

The legal framework surrounding both military and Tribal IDs underscores their significance as trusted forms of identification. Military IDs, being issued by a federal agency, are recognized across all states and are often treated with the same level of scrutiny and respect as a passport or state-issued driver's license. The legal requirements for obtaining a military ID are stringent, as they require proof of service or military affiliation, which is vetted through military records. Similarly, while Tribal IDs are issued by individual tribes, they are also recognized by federal law as proof of identity and tribal membership, provided the tribe is federally recognized. This recognition is important not only for accessing federal programs but also for affirming the legal status of Native American tribes as sovereign nations within the United States. As such, both military and Tribal IDs occupy a unique space in the broader context of legal identification, providing proof of both personal identity and specific legal or sovereign status.

The consequences of improper verification of military and Tribal IDs can be significant. As discussed in previous sections on the importance of accurate ID verification and the legal requirements tied to verifying government-issued IDs, failing to correctly verify these types of IDs can lead to serious legal and practical consequences. For military personnel, improper verification might result in denied access to military benefits, services, or facilities, potentially affecting their healthcare, financial security, and even their legal rights as veterans or active-duty members. In civilian contexts, improperly verified military IDs could lead to fraud, such as individuals falsely claiming military discounts or privileges. For Native American individuals, improper verification of Tribal IDs could prevent them from accessing essential healthcare services, education benefits, or legal rights tied to their tribal membership and land. The significance of these IDs in affirming both identity and status cannot be overstated, and it is essential that those responsible for verifying IDs understand the specific features and legal protections that apply to military and Tribal IDs.

Given their importance in various verification processes, it is crucial for individuals and organizations tasked with ID verification to be familiar with the specific features of military and Tribal IDs. Military IDs, with their standardized design and extensive security features, are often easier to verify, especially in contexts where familiarity with these documents is common, such as in government agencies or large retail chains that offer military discounts. However, for institutions that may be less familiar with Tribal IDs, additional care may be required to ensure that these documents are properly verified. This may involve familiarizing oneself with the specific designs and security features used by the tribes within a given region, as well as understanding the legal recognition that Tribal IDs hold under both state and federal law.

The use of advanced security features in military and Tribal IDs also mirrors the broader trends in identity verification that we have discussed in earlier sections, such as the use of biometrics and electronic chips in passports and the implementation of security features in driver's licenses and non-driver IDs under the REAL ID Act. Both military and Tribal IDs reflect the increasing emphasis on secure, tamper-proof identification in the modern era, where the risks of identity theft and fraud are ever-present. As with other government-issued IDs, the ability to verify these documents accurately and efficiently is critical not only for protecting the rights and privileges of the individuals who hold them but also for maintaining the integrity of the systems and services that rely on secure identification.

Military and Tribal IDs represent two distinct but equally important forms of identification within the U.S. identification system. While they serve different communities and purposes—one affirming military service and the other tribal membership—they are both critical in verifying identity and ensuring access to rights and benefits. The high level of security embedded in these IDs reflects their importance, and the legal frameworks that govern their issuance and use ensure that they are recognized and respected in a wide range of contexts. As we have explored in previous sections, the process of verifying government-issued IDs is essential to upholding the law, preventing fraud, and protecting the rights of individuals. In the case of military and Tribal IDs, accurate verification not only ensures that individuals are recognized for their service or membership but also upholds the broader integrity of the identification system as a whole.

CHAPTER 3

TECHNOLOGICAL ADVANCES IN ID VERIFICATION

DIGITAL AND MOBILE IDS

Digital and mobile IDs are increasingly becoming integral to identification and verification processes in the United States. These modern identification methods are electronic versions of traditional physical IDs like driver's licenses or state-issued ID cards, but they offer enhanced convenience, security, and functionality. Digital IDs are stored on electronic devices such as smartphones or tablets, making them easily accessible for individuals on the go, while mobile IDs refer to digital versions of identification specifically designed for use on mobile devices. As digital transformation continues to impact various sectors, including government services, banking, and transportation, digital and mobile IDs are gaining momentum as trusted and secure alternatives to physical IDs.

In a previous section, the importance of accuracy and authenticity in ID verification was discussed at length. Traditional forms of identification rely on physical elements such as holograms, watermarks, and barcodes to ensure their validity. These features are crucial for visual inspection and machine reading at various checkpoints, from airports to bars. Digital and mobile IDs have transformed this verification process by adding an additional layer of digital security that cannot be easily replicated. For instance, many mobile ID platforms utilize encryption and biometric authentication, such as fingerprint recognition or facial scanning, to verify the identity of the user. This advanced security minimizes the risk of fraudulent activities, which have been more common with physical IDs. Unlike conventional IDs that can be lost, stolen, or counterfeited, digital IDs are harder to tamper with due to encryption techniques and multi-factor authentication protocols.

Another key advantage of digital and mobile IDs is their flexibility. Traditional state-issued IDs are often tied to physical cards, which need to be carried around at all times. Digital and mobile IDs, however, are stored on personal devices, making them easy to access without carrying an extra card. This can be particularly useful in situations where a physical ID might be forgotten or lost, but the individual's smartphone is still readily available. In addition, mobile IDs can be updated and synced with various databases in real-time, ensuring that the information is always current. For example, if a driver changes their address or renews their license, these updates can be automatically reflected in their mobile ID. This feature significantly reduces the lag between changes in personal information and their reflection on identification documents, enhancing the reliability and accuracy of the verification process.

A critical point mentioned earlier is the concern surrounding the security of personal information. Traditional physical IDs, while secure in many ways, carry a risk of exposure. If lost or stolen, they contain all the necessary information for identity theft. Digital and mobile IDs offer a much more secure alternative in this regard. They are designed to provide only the necessary information to the verifying party. For example, when proving age at a bar or event, the mobile ID can show only the date of birth or a confirmation of the individual being over a certain age, without revealing other personal details like home address or full name. This selective sharing of information adds an extra layer of privacy protection, which is a crucial advantage in today's data-driven world where individuals are increasingly concerned about how their personal data is used.

While the convenience and security of digital and mobile IDs are clear, it is essential to recognize that their adoption depends heavily on state and institutional acceptance. Each U.S. state has its own set of guidelines and regulations for issuing and accepting digital IDs. Currently, some states have fully embraced mobile ID programs, while others are in various stages of testing and implementation. This means that the extent to which individuals can rely on mobile IDs may vary depending on their location. For instance, certain states allow the use of digital IDs for law enforcement checks, while others may not yet accept them for formal identification purposes. This reflects the ongoing evolution of digital identity systems and the need for greater standardization across the country.

Building on the section from a previous section regarding the need for ID verification systems to adapt to the changing landscape of digital technology, it's important to highlight how government agencies and private companies are collaborating to create standardized digital ID solutions. Organizations such as the American Association of Motor Vehicle Administrators (AAMVA) and other key stakeholders are working to develop guidelines that ensure the secure issuance and verification of mobile IDs. These collaborations are aimed at establishing interoperable systems that allow digital IDs to be accepted across state lines and different sectors, which would ultimately enhance the usability and trustworthiness of these digital credentials. In many ways, this reflects the broader push towards a more integrated and cohesive national identity system, making ID verification not only more secure but also more user-friendly.

Despite the significant progress in this area, there are challenges that need to be addressed for digital and mobile IDs to reach their full potential. One of the primary concerns is accessibility. While smartphones are ubiquitous, there are still portions of the population, particularly in lower-income or elderly demographics, who may not have regular access to mobile devices or may not be comfortable using them for identification purposes. Additionally, technological barriers such as poor internet connectivity or limited device storage could hinder the effective use of mobile IDs in some cases. In response to this, states and institutions are working on developing alternative solutions, such as providing physical backup cards or offering educational programs to ensure that everyone can take advantage of this technology without being left behind.

A significant challenge discussed earlier in the context of physical ID verification was the process of ensuring that the person presenting the ID matches the individual it was issued to. Mobile IDs address this concern by incorporating biometric authentication methods that are difficult to forge or misrepresent. Fingerprint scans, facial recognition, and other forms of biometrics provide additional confirmation that the person accessing the mobile ID is indeed the rightful owner. This mitigates the risk of someone fraudulently using another person's identification. The combination of biometric verification with encrypted digital IDs creates a multi-layered security framework that significantly improves upon traditional physical identification methods.

The future of digital and mobile IDs is promising, but it also comes with responsibilities for both users and institutions. Individuals must ensure that their devices are secure, regularly updated, and protected with strong passwords or biometric locks. Meanwhile, institutions responsible for issuing and verifying mobile IDs must continuously update their security protocols to defend against evolving cyber threats. There is a growing recognition that digital and mobile IDs are not just a convenience but an essential part of modern identification infrastructure. Their widespread adoption is likely to enhance the efficiency, security, and accuracy of ID verification processes in the coming years.

Digital and mobile IDs represent a significant step forward in the evolution of identification and verification processes. They offer enhanced security features through encryption and biometrics, greater flexibility, and more control over personal information. However, for them to become fully integrated into daily life, there must be continued efforts to standardize systems across states, address accessibility challenges, and ensure ongoing technological improvements. These advancements align closely with the broader section of modernizing ID verification systems, which was emphasized in earlier sections, demonstrating how technology is reshaping the future of secure identification in the United States.

BARCODES, MAGNETIC STRIPS, AND QR CODES

Barcodes, magnetic strips, and QR codes have become vital components of modern identification systems. They play a significant role in the verification process, enhancing the functionality of state-issued identification cards across the United States. These technologies allow quick and accurate scanning of ID information, making it easier for various institutions to confirm the authenticity of an ID and the identity of its bearer. Understanding how these elements work, their significance, and how they are integrated into state ID systems is crucial for both individuals and organizations involved in ID verification processes.

Barcodes, found on most modern state IDs, are machine-readable codes that store a significant amount of data in a compact format. They are composed of a series of parallel lines of varying widths and spaces, and they represent encoded information that can be scanned electronically. The primary function of a barcode on a state ID is to provide a quick and reliable way for a machine to access the information stored on the card, such as the name, date of birth, address, and other relevant details of the ID holder. The data stored in barcodes is typically encrypted, making it difficult for unauthorized individuals to read or manipulate the information without proper access.

The integration of barcodes into state IDs has streamlined the process of verifying identification across various sectors, including law enforcement, retail, and banking. For instance, in the context of a traffic stop, a police officer can quickly scan the barcode on a driver's license to retrieve the necessary information without manually inputting details. This reduces the risk of human error and speeds up the process, ensuring that the officer can focus on verifying the legitimacy of the ID rather than spending time entering data. Additionally, barcodes have become an essential feature for businesses that require age verification, such as liquor stores or casinos. In such cases, scanning the barcode allows the business to quickly confirm whether the individual is of legal age, reducing the potential for underage sales or entry.

In a previous section, the section of traditional ID verification methods emphasized the importance of accuracy in capturing and verifying data. While human eyes are trained to detect common security features like watermarks or holograms, barcodes offer a digital layer of verification that is far less prone to manipulation or error. One of the key strengths of barcodes is their simplicity combined with security. They allow large amounts of information to be accessed quickly while ensuring that the data remains secure and unaltered. Barcodes are particularly advantageous in situations where time is of the essence, such as at airports, where passengers need to be processed rapidly while maintaining high standards of security.

Magnetic strips, another essential element of many state-issued IDs, serve a similar purpose but with a different technology. These strips, often located on the back of an ID card, store data magnetically, much like a traditional credit card. When swiped through a reader, the magnetic strip transmits the encoded information to the system, allowing for quick access to the ID holder's details. While magnetic strips have been in use for several decades, they remain a vital part of modern ID systems due to their durability and capacity to hold various types of data. This makes them particularly useful in environments where IDs are frequently handled, such as in government agencies or large institutions.

In comparison to barcodes, magnetic strips have a slightly different set of strengths. Because they require physical contact with a reader, they are less vulnerable to accidental scanning or interference from other devices. This can be an advantage in high-security environments where it is crucial that only authorized individuals gain access. Furthermore, magnetic strips are more resilient against physical damage than barcodes, which may become unreadable if scratched or smudged. However, like barcodes, the information on magnetic strips is typically encrypted, making it difficult for unauthorized users to access or alter the data without the appropriate technology.

Earlier sections highlighted the evolution of ID technologies and the shift towards more secure and efficient systems. Magnetic strips fit well within this broader narrative, offering a durable and reliable method for storing and accessing personal information on state IDs. They provide a balance between security and ease of use, and they continue to be widely accepted as a standard feature on most state-issued identification cards.

In recent years, QR codes have also emerged as a crucial feature in the world of identification. These two-dimensional barcodes consist of black and white squares arranged in a grid pattern, and they can store a larger amount of data than traditional barcodes. QR codes are particularly advantageous in digital environments, where they can be scanned using smartphones or other devices to quickly access complex datasets. As state and federal institutions increasingly adopt digital ID systems, QR codes have become an important tool for linking physical IDs with digital databases.

One of the major benefits of QR codes is their versatility. Unlike barcodes, which can only be scanned in one direction, QR codes can be read from multiple angles, making them more efficient in a variety of scanning scenarios. They can store more complex information, such as links to government databases, additional security features, or even encrypted data that requires specific authorization to access. QR codes are already being used in some state ID systems to provide a secondary layer of verification, linking physical ID cards to an online profile or government database that contains more detailed personal information.

The integration of QR codes into ID systems aligns with the growing trend of mobile and digital identification, a topic previously covered in detail. As more states explore the use of digital IDs stored on smartphones or tablets, QR codes provide a convenient bridge between physical and digital verification methods. For instance, when someone presents a state-issued digital ID, a QR code embedded in the digital ID can be scanned to verify its authenticity, linking it directly to the issuing authority's secure database. This adds another layer of security, ensuring that even if a digital ID is compromised, it can be easily deactivated or updated within the system.

While QR codes offer numerous benefits, they also come with certain challenges, particularly when it comes to standardization and acceptance. Not all scanners are equipped to read QR codes, especially older machines that were designed to handle traditional barcodes or magnetic strips. This means that while QR codes provide a more advanced solution, they may not yet be fully integrated across all verification systems. However, as the use of QR codes continues to grow, there is a strong push towards greater standardization and the upgrading of scanning technologies to ensure widespread compatibility.

Reflecting on previous sections that emphasized the importance of security in ID verification, it is evident that the combination of barcodes, magnetic strips, and QR codes provides a robust framework for modern state IDs. These elements work together to create a system that is secure, efficient, and adaptable to both physical and digital environments. Each of these technologies offers its own strengths, and when integrated into a comprehensive ID system, they significantly reduce the risk of fraud, ensure faster verification times, and offer a higher level of security for personal information.

Barcodes, magnetic strips, and QR codes are essential components of state-issued identification in the United States, contributing to a more secure and efficient system for verifying identities. Each technology brings unique advantages to the ID verification process, from the simplicity and reliability of barcodes to the durability of magnetic strips and the versatility of QR codes. As technology continues to evolve, these elements will likely remain integral to the future of identification, providing the foundation for a system that can meet the demands of both physical and digital verification. The ongoing advancements in ID technology, as previously discussed, are reshaping the landscape of identification, ensuring that security, efficiency, and adaptability remain at the forefront of state ID systems.

PART 2

Comprehensive Guide to US State IDs (State by State)

CHAPTER 4

HOW TO READ STATE IDS

COMMON ELEMENTS ACROSS ALL STATE IDS

State-issued identification cards in the United States, while varying slightly from one state to another in design, format, and layout, share a range of common elements that are essential for their purpose in identity verification. These standardized features ensure consistency across different jurisdictions, allowing businesses, law enforcement, and government agencies to effectively recognize and verify the authenticity of IDs, regardless of where they are issued. Understanding the common elements that appear on all state IDs is fundamental to grasping how these cards function in various contexts, from routine age verification to more complex security screenings.

One of the most crucial components found on all state IDs is personal information that identifies the cardholder. This includes the individual's full legal name, photograph, date of birth, and residential address. These key details are essential in ensuring that the cardholder can be accurately identified, whether for simple transactions such as purchasing alcohol or for more sensitive procedures like boarding an airplane. The inclusion of the cardholder's name and photograph provides immediate visual verification, while the date of birth is used to determine eligibility for age-restricted activities. The residential address, while not always required for every transaction, is a critical detail that can be cross-checked in various situations, such as when verifying the identity of a voter or processing a bank application.

In a previous section, the role of personal data security and accuracy in ID verification was discussed, emphasizing how secure storage and presentation of such information help prevent identity theft and fraud. State IDs reflect this principle by incorporating high levels of security in the way this information is presented. Many states now require additional verification steps when issuing an ID to ensure that the personal details included on the card are accurate and up-to-date. This often involves cross-referencing government databases and requiring proof of residency, further ensuring that each ID is legitimate and linked to the correct individual.

In addition to personal information, all state IDs include a unique identification number, often referred to as the ID number or driver's license number. This number serves as a key reference point in various systems and databases used for verification purposes. Whether law enforcement is pulling up a driving record or a business is checking identification for age verification, the ID number allows access to additional records and data that are tied to the individual. Importantly, the ID number is unique to the cardholder and is linked to other important information, such as prior convictions, driving history, or immigration status, depending on the database being accessed. This feature not only ensures that the cardholder's history can be easily retrieved but also helps prevent fraud, as the number can be flagged in instances of stolen or counterfeit IDs.

Security features that are embedded into the physical structure of state IDs are also consistent across all jurisdictions, though they may vary in exact design or format. These include holograms, watermarks, UV images, microprinting, and laser engraving. These elements serve the dual purpose of verifying authenticity and preventing counterfeiting. Holograms and watermarks, for example, are difficult to replicate and can be easily checked using light or simple tools available to security personnel or ID checkers. UV images, which are only visible under ultraviolet light, provide another layer of security, as they allow for a secondary verification that is not visible to the naked eye. Microprinting and laser engraving are also common across state IDs, adding intricate details that are nearly impossible to duplicate with conventional printing methods.

The importance of these security features was previously highlighted when discussing the evolution of ID verification technologies. As the use of digital and mobile IDs grows, the necessity for secure, tamper-resistant elements on physical IDs remains just as important. Security features on physical IDs help prevent identity theft and fraudulent activities, while also ensuring that the cardholder is who they claim to be. In situations where digital IDs might not yet be accepted or fully integrated, the physical card's security features play a critical role in maintaining trust and integrity in identification systems.

Another universally shared feature across state IDs is the inclusion of the issuing state's name and relevant jurisdictional details. Typically, state IDs display the name of the state prominently at the top of the card, ensuring that anyone checking the ID knows where it was issued. This is particularly important when verifying IDs across state lines, as different states may have slightly different rules and requirements for ID issuance. Having the state name clearly displayed ensures that ID checkers can easily recognize the card's origin, which is especially important when working with a national system of identification. In some cases, state IDs may also include additional jurisdictional details, such as the name of the specific county or municipality where the card was issued, though this is less common than the state name itself.

Additionally, the expiration date is another critical element that appears on all state IDs. The expiration date serves several important functions. First, it ensures that the cardholder's information remains current. As people move, change names, or reach different legal milestones, their identification needs to be updated to reflect those changes. By requiring that state IDs be renewed periodically, the expiration date provides a mechanism to ensure that individuals update their information regularly. This reduces the likelihood of outdated or inaccurate information being presented during ID checks. Second, the expiration date allows businesses and government agencies to confirm that the ID is still valid. Using an expired ID can present risks, as it might no longer reflect the current status of the cardholder, and businesses are often prohibited from accepting such IDs for legal transactions, such as purchasing alcohol or boarding a flight.

In relation to the previous section of how digital and mobile IDs are becoming more prevalent, it's worth noting that expiration dates still play a vital role in both physical and digital formats. Whether an ID is stored in a mobile app or carried as a physical card, regular renewal processes are essential to ensuring that the data remains up-to-date and that any technological or legal changes are reflected in the ID itself. In both cases, the expiration date signals the need for renewal and continued verification of identity, maintaining the integrity of the system.

State IDs also universally feature some form of signature from the cardholder. The signature serves as an additional layer of verification, allowing businesses or government agencies to cross-reference the signature on the ID with other documents, such as credit card receipts or contracts. While signatures can be forged, they still provide a personal verification method that remains common across all state-issued IDs. The presence of a signature on an ID reinforces its use as a legal document and provides one more layer of security in the verification process.

Some state IDs also include endorsements or restrictions specific to the cardholder's circumstances, such as whether they are licensed to drive a specific class of vehicle or if there are any medical conditions that could affect their ability to operate a vehicle. While not all state IDs display this information in the same way, it is a common feature across the country, particularly on driver's licenses. These endorsements or restrictions can be important in situations where the ID is being used for specific purposes, such as when applying for a job that requires driving, or for medical professionals who need to understand a patient's health condition.

The common elements shared by state IDs across the United States are foundational to the reliability, security, and functionality of the identification system. These elements, including personal information, unique ID numbers, security features, the issuing state, expiration dates, and cardholder signatures, work together to create a standardized and trustworthy ID system. These features ensure that state-issued IDs can be effectively used for a wide range of verification purposes, from everyday transactions to more complex legal and governmental procedures. As discussed in earlier sections, the future of identification will likely continue to evolve, particularly with the rise of digital and mobile IDs, but the core elements of personal identification, security, and verification will remain central to the system's integrity and effectiveness.

VARIATIONS IN DESIGN, SECURITY FEATURES, AND DATA POINTS

State-issued identification cards in the United States, while governed by federal standards for accuracy and security, exhibit significant variations in design, security features, and data points. These differences reflect each state's unique approach to balancing aesthetic design, ease of use, and security. Understanding these variations is crucial for anyone involved in ID verification, as recognizing the distinctions can help identify potential inconsistencies that may point to fraudulent or tampered IDs. Moreover, despite these differences, all state IDs aim to fulfill the same essential function: to provide a reliable, secure means of identifying individuals.

The design of state IDs is one area where considerable variation exists. Each state typically incorporates symbols or images that reflect its identity or heritage, making the card distinctive and recognizable. For example, California's driver's license may feature the iconic image of the Golden Gate Bridge, while Florida's ID might include a graphic of a palm tree or the state seal. These design elements not only give the ID a unique appearance but also serve to ensure that the card can be easily recognized as legitimate within its state of issuance. The use of state-specific imagery contributes to the visual security of the card, as fraudulent IDs often fail to replicate the exact color schemes, fonts, or design details that are native to the issuing state. While these design elements may seem purely aesthetic, they are, in fact, an integral part of the identification process, helping those who are tasked with verifying IDs to quickly assess the legitimacy of the card.

In a previous section, the common elements shared across all state IDs were explored, focusing on the core features like personal information, the issuing state's name, and expiration dates. While these elements provide a foundation, the variation in state ID design introduces another layer of complexity. Each state's decision to emphasize certain design features over others can influence the ease with which an ID is verified. For instance, some states opt for brighter, more colorful designs that make the card stand out, while others use more subdued tones that focus heavily on the placement of security features.

Security features, though universally present on state IDs, are another area where significant variation occurs. While certain security elements such as holograms, microprinting, and watermarks are common across most IDs, the specific implementation of these features varies widely from state to state. Some states employ highly complex holographic overlays that shift color and image depending on the angle from which they are viewed, while others use more straightforward holograms featuring the state seal or emblem. These holographic elements are designed to prevent counterfeiting by making it difficult to replicate the exact patterns and shifts in light that are present on the legitimate card. The complexity of these holograms can vary depending on the state, with some employing multiple layers of holographic design to add extra security.

Microprinting, another common security feature, is typically used to display text or patterns that are too small to be reproduced by conventional printing methods. This fine print is often placed in areas of the card that are less obvious, requiring a closer inspection to verify. While the use of microprinting is common, the specific placement and content of the microtext vary between states. Some states choose to incorporate their name or abbreviation in microprint, while others may include security codes or other hidden text that can be used during the verification process.

In some states, microprinting is strategically placed near the photo or signature area to make tampering with these critical data points more difficult.

Watermarks and UV features also vary from state to state. Watermarks, which are typically visible only when held up to light, can feature state seals, emblems, or other symbolic imagery. The design and placement of these watermarks are unique to each state, making them another key component in verifying the authenticity of an ID. UV features, which are only visible under ultraviolet light, often include additional information or images that provide a secondary layer of verification. In some states, the UV features may include the individual's date of birth or a duplicate image of their photo, while in others, these features might include the state's name or additional security codes.

Despite the variations in security features, all states strive to incorporate elements that prevent forgery and tampering. As discussed earlier, the goal of ID security is to ensure that both physical and digital elements are difficult to replicate or alter without detection. The combination of holograms, microprinting, watermarks, and UV features creates a multi-layered defense against counterfeiting. Each of these elements serves a unique purpose in the verification process, and their variation across states reflects the balance each state must strike between ease of use, cost, and security.

Another area where state IDs differ is in the data points they include. While all IDs contain basic information such as name, date of birth, and residential address, the specific data points can vary depending on the state's regulations and the type of ID issued. Some states, for example, include more detailed information on their IDs, such as gender, height, eye color, and hair color, while others may focus on only the most essential data points. This variation can be particularly important in situations where a more detailed physical description is necessary for identification purposes, such as in law enforcement or security screenings.

In some cases, state IDs may include additional data points for specific purposes. For instance, driver's licenses often include information about any restrictions or endorsements related to the individual's driving privileges, such as whether they are permitted to drive certain types of vehicles or if they are required to wear corrective lenses. In contrast, non-driver state IDs may omit these driving-related details, focusing solely on personal identification information. Additionally, some states include a designation for organ donor status, while others include information about veteran status or other special categories that may be relevant to the cardholder's identity.

The inclusion of different data points on state IDs is not just a matter of state preference, but often reflects the specific needs and laws of each state. For instance, some states require IDs to display additional information related to voting eligibility, while others may emphasize information related to immigration status or residency. These variations ensure that the ID meets the legal and functional requirements of the issuing state while maintaining consistency in its core purpose of providing a secure means of identification.

These variations in data points also tie back to the section of common elements across state IDs. While the foundational components of a state ID remain the same, the way in which each state chooses to represent or include additional information can vary significantly. This makes it essential for ID checkers to be familiar with the specific requirements and formats used in different states. For example, while one state may prominently display the organ donor designation at the bottom of the card, another may integrate it into the background design or include it as a small icon near the photo.

One particularly important distinction among state IDs is the variation in how Real ID compliance is displayed. Real ID, a federal standard for identification that was introduced to improve security, is denoted differently on state IDs. Some states use a gold or black star to signify that the ID is Real ID-compliant, while others may include additional text or symbols to indicate compliance. This is particularly relevant for individuals who need to use their ID for federal purposes, such as boarding a domestic flight or entering federal facilities. Understanding how each state marks its Real ID-compliant cards is essential in ensuring that the ID is accepted in these contexts.

While state IDs across the United States share core elements, the variations in design, security features, and data points introduce a level of complexity that is essential to understand in ID verification. These differences reflect each state's approach to balancing security with functionality, ensuring that the ID serves its purpose while preventing fraud and forgery. As previously discussed, the goal of state IDs is to provide a secure, reliable means of identification, and these variations help maintain the integrity of the system while accommodating the specific needs and laws of each state. Understanding these differences is critical for anyone involved in the verification process, as recognizing the unique features of each state's ID can help prevent errors and ensure that identification is accurately and securely verified.

STATE-SPECIFIC ID FORMATS

State-issued identification cards across the United States, while unified in their core purpose of verifying identity, vary significantly in their formats, designs, and physical features. Each state adopts a distinct approach to how its ID cards look and feel, incorporating state-specific symbols, security features, and data formats. Understanding these variations in state-specific ID formats is critical for effective ID verification, as it ensures accuracy in identifying legitimate cards and helps in detecting potential counterfeits.

Here's a detailed description of the state-specific ID formats for each state, organized into a paragraph-based, descriptive approach rather than itemized lists, but following the structure of a table, as requested:

State	Design and Visible Features	Security Features
Alabama	Alabama's ID features a white background with a subtle outline of the state. A blue banner at the top displays the state name. The individual's photograph is positioned on the left-hand side, with personal information placed below.	A holographic state seal overlay reflects light, making it difficult to counterfeit. The card also includes UV-sensitive features visible under ultraviolet light, adding an additional layer of

		security for verification purposes.
Alaska	The design is centered around the state's natural scenery, featuring an image of the Northern Lights as a backdrop. The cardholder's photo is placed on the right, with the state name prominently displayed in a dark blue banner at the top.	A holographic image of the Alaska state flag, which shifts in color depending on the angle of light, acts as a key security measure. UV elements, such as a state emblem, also become visible under UV light, allowing for secondary verification.
Arizona	Arizona's ID includes a light tan background with desert landscapes and cactus imagery, embodying the state's geography. The cardholder's photograph is on the top left, with personal data neatly arranged.	The state seal is displayed as a copper-colored hologram, along with microprinting in the background, making it highly resistant to forgery. Under UV light, the Arizona state flag and

		Grand Canyon outline are visible for added protection against counterfeiting.
Arkansas	Arkansas IDs feature a clean white background with a small depiction of the state flag in the upper left. The card layout is simple and easy to read, with personal data well spaced out.	Holographic images of the state seal appear across the surface, and UV-sensitive elements, such as the repeating outline of the state, become visible under ultraviolet light, ensuring the card's legitimacy and helping to prevent fraud.
California	California's ID card prominently features the Golden Gate Bridge in the background. The state name appears in bold at the top, while the cardholder's information is displayed in a well-organized layout, with their photo on the left side.	A multi-layered holographic overlay with the California state bear and star symbols shifts with changing light angles. UV features include a duplicate

		image of the cardholder's photo and the California bear emblem, visible only under UV light, making it one of the most secure IDs in the country.
Colorado	Colorado's ID design is marked by a scenic mountain range in the background, with the state name in large, bold white letters at the top. The cardholder's photo is located on the left, with personal details arranged in an orderly fashion.	The use of translucent ink creates an overlay of the state emblem that is visible only at certain angles. UV-sensitive images, including a mountain range outline, become visible when viewed under ultraviolet light, serving as a tool for ensuring the ID's authenticity.
Connecticut	Connecticut's ID features a solid blue background with the state name clearly displayed at the top. The cardholder's photo is	The state seal is embedded as a hologram on the card's surface, and

	positioned on the left, with their personal details evenly distributed.	fine microprinting is used throughout the card design, making it difficult to replicate. Under UV light, additional security features such as the state flag are visible, adding another verification layer during inspections.
Delaware	Delaware's ID features a light background with a depiction of the Delaware River. The state name is prominently displayed at the top, and the cardholder's details are arranged in a clear and simple layout, with their photo located to the left.	Holographic overlays of the state seal and microprinted patterns make it difficult for counterfeiters to duplicate. Under UV light, hidden images such as a duplicate photo of the cardholder appear, adding a further layer of security for validation checks.

Florida	Florida's ID uses vibrant colors, featuring a backdrop of palm trees and ocean waves to reflect the state's tropical environment. The state name is displayed in bright orange letters at the top, and the cardholder's photo is placed on the left side.	A multicolored holographic overlay features intricate patterns and the state seal, which shifts in color depending on the viewing angle. UV-sensitive images of palm trees and the Florida state flag are embedded into the card, visible only under UV light, further securing the card from counterfeiting attempts.
Georgia	Georgia's ID has a peach-colored background with subtle illustrations of peaches, paying homage to the state's nickname. The state name is displayed in bold white letters at the top, and the cardholder's information is arranged neatly, with the photo on the left.	A holographic peach overlay reflects under light, alongside a repeating microprint pattern of the state motto. The card also includes UV elements, with

		the state's outline becoming visible under ultraviolet light, providing an added layer of authenticity when inspected.
Hawaii	Hawaii's ID features a tropical design with palm trees and ocean imagery in the background. The state name appears at the top in bold blue letters, with the cardholder's photo positioned on the right. The personal details are laid out cleanly across the card.	A hologram of a Hawaiian lei can be seen when the card is tilted, alongside microprinted patterns. UV features include hidden tropical images like palm trees, which only appear under ultraviolet light, allowing verification officers to confirm the card's legitimacy during checks.
Idaho	Idaho's ID card adopts a rustic design with a backdrop of mountains and forests. The state name is displayed at the top in white capital letters. The cardholder's	A holographic overlay featuring the state seal is visible under

	photograph is located on the left, and personal information is displayed in a simple, easy-to-read format.	light. Additionally, UV-sensitive images of a mountain range and state emblem are embedded within the card, adding a second layer of protection when exposed to ultraviolet light, making it challenging to forge.
Illinois	Illinois' ID design incorporates a depiction of the Chicago skyline in the background, with the state name prominently displayed at the top in bold letters. The cardholder's photograph is on the left side, and personal details are neatly distributed across the card.	A multicolored hologram of the state flag is embedded across the surface of the card, which shifts in appearance depending on the angle of light. Microprinting and UV-sensitive elements, including a hidden image of the state capitol building,

		become visible under ultraviolet light, providing added layers of verification.
Indiana	Indiana's ID card has a blue background with a faint image of the state flag. The state name appears at the top in capital letters, and the cardholder's photo is positioned on the left, with the rest of the personal data displayed clearly.	The card includes a holographic overlay of the state's torch emblem, alongside fine microprinting that is nearly impossible to replicate. UV-sensitive features, such as a hidden image of the state seal, appear under ultraviolet light, serving as a key measure in confirming the authenticity of the ID.
Iowa	Iowa's ID features an agricultural theme, with a background of rolling plains and farmland. The state name is displayed in bold white letters at the top, with the cardholder's photograph on the left and the rest	The state seal appears as a holographic overlay, shifting in color under light.

	of the information clearly visible below.	Additionally, a repeating pattern of microprinting ensures the ID is difficult to forge. Under UV light, a duplicate image of the cardholder's photo, along with state-specific symbols, becomes visible, providing additional security against counterfeiting.
Kansas	Kansas' ID features a landscape of wheat fields and open skies in the background. The state name appears at the top in bold letters, and the cardholder's information is clearly laid out with the photograph on the right side.	A holographic sunflower, the state flower, is embedded within the card's surface, which reflects light when tilted. UV-sensitive images of the state outline and the Kansas state flag are embedded within the

		card and are only visible when exposed to ultraviolet light, offering additional protection against counterfeiting attempts.
Kentucky	Kentucky's ID design incorporates a background of rolling hills and horses, symbolizing the state's equestrian heritage. The state name is displayed at the top in capital letters, with the cardholder's photo on the left and the personal details spread across the card.	A holographic overlay of the state seal, alongside fine microprinting, makes the ID difficult to replicate. Additionally, UV-sensitive features, including hidden images of horse motifs and the state outline, appear under ultraviolet light, ensuring the card's legitimacy during verification processes.
Louisiana	Louisiana's ID features a scenic background with swamps and bayous, reflective of the state's geography. The state name is prominently displayed at the top,	A hologram of the state seal overlays the card's surface, shimmering

	with the cardholder's photo on the right-hand side.	when viewed at different angles. Fine microprinting and UV-sensitive elements, such as hidden images of the state bird, become visible under UV light, offering enhanced protection against fraudulent replication.
Maine	Maine's ID incorporates images of pine trees and forest landscapes, reflecting the state's natural environment. The state name appears at the top in large letters, with the cardholder's photo positioned on the left side of the card.	A holographic overlay of the state seal, combined with intricate microprinting patterns, helps prevent forgery. Under UV light, images of pine trees and the state outline become visible, adding a secondary method of verification when

		examining the card's authenticity.
Maryland	Maryland's ID features the state flag as a prominent design element, with the cardholder's photograph on the left and personal details arranged in a clear layout. The state name is displayed at the top in bold letters.	A multicolored holographic image of the state flag and a crab emblem are embedded within the card's surface. UV-sensitive features include the state capitol building and a duplicate image of the cardholder's photograph, which are only visible under ultraviolet light, providing enhanced protection against forgery.
Massachusetts	Massachusetts' ID card incorporates an image of the state capitol building as a background. The state name is prominently displayed at the top, and the cardholder's personal information is clearly visible, with the photo on the left-hand side.	A holographic overlay of the state seal appears on the card, shifting when viewed from different angles. Microprinting

		adds an extra layer of protection, while UV-sensitive images of the state flag and hidden elements, such as a duplicate photo of the cardholder, become visible when viewed under ultraviolet light.
Michigan	Michigan's ID design features an image of the Mackinac Bridge in the background. The state name appears in bold letters at the top, and the cardholder's information is clearly laid out with the photograph on the left side.	A holographic overlay of the state flag and an outline of the Mackinac Bridge shimmer when the card is tilted. Fine microprinting ensures the card is difficult to replicate, and UV-sensitive elements, such as hidden state symbols, become visible when exposed to ultraviolet

		light, providing added protection against counterfeiting attempts.
Minnesota	Minnesota's ID includes a scenic background of lakes and trees, representing the state's natural beauty. The state name is displayed at the top, and the cardholder's photo is positioned on the left.	The card features a holographic overlay of the state seal, which reflects under light. Microprinting adds an extra layer of protection against fraud. UV-sensitive images of the state's lakes and a duplicate photo of the cardholder are visible under ultraviolet light, making it difficult for counterfeiters to create convincing forgeries.
Mississippi	Mississippi's ID card incorporates a background image of the state capitol building. The state name appears in bold letters at the top, and the cardholder's personal	A holographic image of the state seal and a repeating microprinted

	information is neatly arranged with the photograph on the left.	pattern of the state name are embedded across the surface of the card. UV-sensitive features, such as hidden images of the state outline, appear under ultraviolet light, adding an additional layer of protection against counterfeiting.
Missouri	Missouri's ID design features an image of the Gateway Arch in the background, reflecting the state's historical landmarks. The state name is displayed at the top, with the cardholder's personal details clearly laid out, including a photograph on the left side.	A holographic overlay of the state seal shifts colors when viewed at different angles, making it difficult to replicate. Microprinting and UV-sensitive images of the state flag and a duplicate of the cardholder's photograph are embedded

		into the card, offering a dual method of verification to prevent fraud.
Montana	Montana's ID incorporates a background of mountains and prairies, reflecting the state's geography. The state name is prominently displayed at the top, and the cardholder's personal information is clearly visible, with their photo positioned on the right.	A holographic overlay of the state seal and fine microprinting protect against counterfeiting. UV-sensitive images of the state's outline and other state symbols become visible under ultraviolet light, adding an extra layer of protection to ensure the authenticity of the card.
Nebraska	Nebraska's ID card features a scenic background of open plains and farmlands, reflecting the state's agricultural heritage. The state name is prominently displayed at the top in bold letters, with the cardholder's photograph on the left side. The personal information is neatly organized below the photo, ensuring clarity and ease of reading.	A holographic overlay of the state seal is embedded across the card's surface, which shifts colors when tilted. Additionally, microprinting of the state name and a

		repeating pattern of wheat stalks are present to prevent forgery. UV-sensitive elements, such as a hidden outline of the state and additional state symbols, become visible under ultraviolet light, providing an extra layer of security during verification.
Nevada	Nevada's ID features a backdrop of the Las Vegas Strip skyline, incorporating vibrant colors that reflect the state's lively culture. The state name is displayed prominently at the top in gold letters, with the cardholder's photo positioned on the right side. Personal details are clearly listed below the photo, ensuring easy readability.	The card includes a holographic image of the state seal and the Nevada state flag, which shimmer when viewed from different angles. Fine microprinting of the state motto and a repeating pattern of

		casino chips enhance security. UV-sensitive features, such as hidden images of the state's natural landmarks, are embedded within the card and only become visible under ultraviolet light, making the ID difficult to counterfeit.
New Hampshire	New Hampshire's ID card showcases an image of Mount Washington in the background, symbolizing the state's mountainous terrain. The state name is prominently displayed at the top in uppercase letters, with the cardholder's photograph on the left side. Personal information is organized clearly below the photo, maintaining a clean and professional appearance.	A holographic overlay featuring the state seal is present on the card, which changes color when tilted. Microprinting of the state name and a pattern of pine trees adds an additional layer of security. UV-sensitive elements, including hidden images

		of the state's outline and natural landmarks, become visible under ultraviolet light, ensuring the ID's authenticity and preventing forgery.
New Jersey	New Jersey's ID incorporates an urban skyline background, representing the state's bustling cities. The state name is displayed at the top in bold blue letters, with the cardholder's photo on the right side. Personal details are neatly arranged below the photo, ensuring clarity and ease of verification.	The card features a holographic overlay of the state seal and the New Jersey state flag, which shimmer when viewed from different angles. Fine microprinting of the state motto and a repeating pattern of cityscapes enhance security. UV-sensitive features, such as hidden images of the state's landmarks and

		additional state symbols, are embedded within the card and become visible under ultraviolet light, providing an extra layer of protection against counterfeiting.
New Mexico	New Mexico's ID card showcases vibrant Southwestern designs, including adobe-style buildings and desert landscapes. The state name is prominently displayed at the top in bold red letters, with the cardholder's photograph positioned on the left side. Personal information is clearly organized below the photo, maintaining a visually appealing and functional layout.	A holographic overlay of the state seal and the Zia sun symbol is embedded within the card, shifting colors when tilted. Microprinting of the state name and traditional Southwestern patterns add an extra layer of security. UV-sensitive elements, including hidden images of desert flora and fauna, become

		visible under ultraviolet light, ensuring the ID's authenticity and preventing fraudulent replication.
New York	New York's ID features a backdrop of the Statue of Liberty and the New York City skyline, symbolizing the state's iconic landmarks. The state name is displayed at the top in bold white letters against a dark blue banner, with the cardholder's photograph on the right side. Personal details are neatly arranged below the photo for easy readability.	The card includes a holographic overlay of the state seal and the New York state flag, which shimmer when viewed from different angles. Fine microprinting of the state motto and a repeating pattern of skyscrapers enhance security. UV-sensitive features, such as hidden images of the Statue of Liberty and additional state symbols, are embedded within the

		card and become visible under ultraviolet light, providing an extra layer of protection against counterfeiting.
North Carolina	North Carolina's ID card features a scenic background of the Outer Banks and pine forests, reflecting the state's diverse landscapes. The state name is prominently displayed at the top in bold letters, with the cardholder's photograph positioned on the left side. Personal information is clearly organized below the photo, ensuring clarity and ease of verification.	A holographic overlay of the state seal is embedded across the card's surface, which shifts colors when tilted. Microprinting of the state name and a repeating pattern of lighthouse symbols add an additional layer of security. UV-sensitive elements, including hidden images of the state's landmarks and natural features, become visible under

		ultraviolet light, ensuring the ID's authenticity and preventing fraudulent replication.
North Dakota	North Dakota's ID incorporates images of the Great Plains and agricultural fields in the background, symbolizing the state's farming heritage. The state name is displayed at the top in bold green letters, with the cardholder's photograph on the right side. Personal details are neatly arranged below the photo, maintaining a clean and functional layout.	The card features a holographic overlay of the state seal and a repeating pattern of wheat stalks, which shimmer when viewed from different angles. Fine microprinting of the state name and additional agricultural motifs enhance security. UV-sensitive elements, such as hidden images of the state's outline and natural landmarks, become visible under ultraviolet

		light, providing an extra layer of protection against counterfeiting.
Ohio	Ohio's ID card showcases an image of the state's industrial heritage, featuring factories and urban landscapes in the background. The state name is prominently displayed at the top in bold letters, with the cardholder's photograph positioned on the left side. Personal information is clearly organized below the photo, ensuring clarity and ease of verification.	A holographic overlay of the state seal and the Ohio state flag is embedded within the card, shifting colors when tilted. Microprinting of the state name and a repeating pattern of industrial symbols add an additional layer of security. UV-sensitive features, including hidden images of the state's landmarks and natural features, become visible under ultraviolet light, ensuring the ID's

		authenticity and preventing fraudulent replication.
Oklahoma	Oklahoma's ID features a backdrop of the state's natural landscapes, including plains and oil rigs, reflecting its diverse economy. The state name is displayed at the top in bold blue letters, with the cardholder's photograph on the right side. Personal details are neatly arranged below the photo for easy readability.	The card includes a holographic overlay of the state seal and the Oklahoma state flag, which shimmer when viewed from different angles. Fine microprinting of the state name and a repeating pattern of oil rigs enhance security. UV-sensitive elements, such as hidden images of the state's natural features and additional state symbols, are embedded within the card and become visible under ultraviolet light,

		providing an extra layer of protection against counterfeiting.
Oregon	Oregon's ID card showcases images of the state's lush forests and rugged coastlines in the background. The state name is prominently displayed at the top in bold green letters, with the cardholder's photograph on the left side. Personal information is clearly organized below the photo, maintaining a clean and professional appearance.	A holographic overlay of the state seal and the Oregon state flag is embedded within the card, which shifts colors when tilted. Microprinting of the state name and a repeating pattern of forest motifs add an additional layer of security. UV-sensitive features, including hidden images of the state's landmarks and natural features, become visible under ultraviolet light, ensuring the ID's authenticity

		and preventing fraudulent replication.
Pennsylvania	Pennsylvania's ID features a backdrop of the Liberty Bell and Independence Hall, symbolizing the state's historical significance. The state name is displayed at the top in bold letters, with the cardholder's photograph positioned on the right side. Personal details are neatly arranged below the photo for easy readability.	The card includes a holographic overlay of the state seal and the Pennsylvania state flag, which shimmer when viewed from different angles. Fine microprinting of the state name and a repeating pattern of historical symbols enhance security. UV-sensitive elements, such as hidden images of the state's landmarks and additional state symbols, are embedded within the card and become visible under

		ultraviolet light, providing an extra layer of protection against counterfeiting.
Rhode Island	Rhode Island's ID card features a nautical theme, with images of lighthouses and ocean waves in the background. The state name is prominently displayed at the top in bold blue letters, with the cardholder's photograph on the left side. Personal information is clearly organized below the photo, ensuring clarity and ease of verification.	A holographic overlay of the state seal and the Rhode Island state flag is embedded within the card, shifting colors when tilted. Microprinting of the state name and a repeating pattern of lighthouse motifs add an additional layer of security. UV-sensitive features, including hidden images of the state's landmarks and natural features, become visible under ultraviolet

		light, ensuring the ID's authenticity and preventing fraudulent replication.
South Carolina	South Carolina's ID incorporates images of the state's historic plantations and coastal landscapes in the background. The state name is displayed at the top in bold letters, with the cardholder's photograph positioned on the right side. Personal details are neatly arranged below the photo for easy readability.	The card features a holographic overlay of the state seal and the South Carolina state flag, which shimmer when viewed from different angles. Fine microprinting of the state name and a repeating pattern of magnolia flowers enhance security. UV-sensitive elements, such as hidden images of the state's landmarks and additional state symbols, are embedded within the card and

		become visible under ultraviolet light, providing an extra layer of protection against counterfeiting.
South Dakota	South Dakota's ID card showcases the iconic Mount Rushmore in the background, symbolizing the state's historical significance. The state name is prominently displayed at the top in bold letters, with the cardholder's photograph on the left side. Personal information is clearly organized below the photo, ensuring clarity and ease of verification.	A holographic overlay of the state seal and the South Dakota state flag is embedded within the card, which shifts colors when tilted. Microprinting of the state name and a repeating pattern of presidential faces add an additional layer of security. UV-sensitive features, including hidden images of Mount Rushmore and additional state symbols, become

		visible under ultraviolet light, ensuring the ID's authenticity and preventing fraudulent replication.
Tennessee	Tennessee's ID features a backdrop of the Great Smoky Mountains and music symbols, reflecting the state's natural beauty and musical heritage. The state name is displayed at the top in bold red letters, with the cardholder's photograph on the right side. Personal details are neatly arranged below the photo for easy readability.	The card includes a holographic overlay of the state seal and the Tennessee state flag, which shimmer when viewed from different angles. Fine microprinting of the state name and a repeating pattern of musical notes enhance security. UV-sensitive elements, such as hidden images of the state's landmarks and additional state symbols, are embedded within the

		card and become visible under ultraviolet light, providing an extra layer of protection against counterfeiting.
Texas	Texas's ID card showcases a backdrop of the state capitol building and expansive ranch landscapes, reflecting the state's heritage. The state name is prominently displayed at the top in bold letters, with the cardholder's photograph positioned on the left side. Personal information is clearly organized below the photo, maintaining a clean and functional layout.	A holographic overlay of the state seal and the Texas state flag is embedded within the card, which shifts colors when tilted. Microprinting of the state name and a repeating pattern of longhorn cattle add an additional layer of security. UV-sensitive features, including hidden images of the state's landmarks and additional state symbols, become

		visible under ultraviolet light, ensuring the ID's authenticity and preventing fraudulent replication.
Utah	Utah's ID features images of the state's national parks and mountainous landscapes in the background. The state name is displayed at the top in bold white letters against a dark blue banner, with the cardholder's photograph on the right side. Personal details are neatly arranged below the photo, ensuring clarity and ease of verification.	The card includes a holographic overlay of the state seal and the Utah state flag, which shimmer when viewed from different angles. Fine microprinting of the state name and a repeating pattern of mountain motifs enhance security. UV-sensitive elements, such as hidden images of the state's natural features and additional state symbols, are embedded within the

		card and become visible under ultraviolet light, providing an extra layer of protection against counterfeiting.
Vermont	Vermont's ID card showcases a backdrop of rolling hills and maple forests, reflecting the state's natural beauty. The state name is prominently displayed at the top in bold green letters, with the cardholder's photograph positioned on the left side. Personal information is clearly organized below the photo, maintaining a clean and professional appearance.	A holographic overlay of the state seal and the Vermont state flag is embedded within the card, shifting colors when tilted. Microprinting of the state name and a repeating pattern of maple leaves add an additional layer of security. UV-sensitive features, including hidden images of the state's landmarks and additional state symbols, become

		visible under ultraviolet light, ensuring the ID's authenticity and preventing fraudulent replication.
Virginia	Virginia's ID features a backdrop of historical landmarks such as Colonial Williamsburg and Monticello, symbolizing the state's rich history. The state name is displayed at the top in bold blue letters, with the cardholder's photograph on the right side. Personal details are neatly arranged below the photo for easy readability.	The card includes a holographic overlay of the state seal and the Virginia state flag, which shimmer when viewed from different angles. Fine microprinting of the state name and a repeating pattern of historical symbols enhance security. UV-sensitive elements, such as hidden images of the state's landmarks and additional state symbols, are embedded

		within the card and become visible under ultraviolet light, providing an extra layer of protection against counterfeiting.
Washington	Washington's ID card showcases images of the state's natural beauty, including Mount Rainier and evergreen forests, in the background. The state name is prominently displayed at the top in bold green letters, with the cardholder's photograph positioned on the left side. Personal information is clearly organized below the photo, ensuring clarity and ease of verification.	A holographic overlay of the state seal and the Washington state flag is embedded within the card, which shifts colors when tilted. Microprinting of the state name and a repeating pattern of evergreen trees add an additional layer of security. UV-sensitive features, including hidden images of the state's natural landmarks and

		additional state symbols, become visible under ultraviolet light, ensuring the ID's authenticity and preventing fraudulent replication.
West Virginia	West Virginia's ID features a backdrop of the Appalachian Mountains and river landscapes, reflecting the state's geography. The state name is displayed at the top in bold white letters against a dark blue banner, with the cardholder's photograph on the right side. Personal details are neatly arranged below the photo, maintaining a clean and functional layout.	The card includes a holographic overlay of the state seal and the West Virginia state flag, which shimmer when viewed from different angles. Fine microprinting of the state name and a repeating pattern of mountain motifs enhance security. UV-sensitive elements, such as hidden images of the state's natural features and

		additional state symbols, are embedded within the card and become visible under ultraviolet light, providing an extra layer of protection against counterfeiting.
Wisconsin	Wisconsin's ID card showcases images of dairy farms and lakes in the background, reflecting the state's agricultural and natural heritage. The state name is prominently displayed at the top in bold blue letters, with the cardholder's photograph positioned on the left side. Personal information is clearly organized below the photo, ensuring clarity and ease of verification.	A holographic overlay of the state seal and the Wisconsin state flag is embedded within the card, which shifts colors when tilted. Microprinting of the state name and a repeating pattern of dairy motifs add an additional layer of security. UV-sensitive features, including hidden images of the state's

		landmarks and additional state symbols, become visible under ultraviolet light, ensuring the ID's authenticity and preventing fraudulent replication.
Wyoming	Wyoming's ID features a backdrop of the Grand Tetons and open plains, symbolizing the state's natural beauty. The state name is displayed at the top in bold white letters against a dark green banner, with the cardholder's photograph on the right side. Personal details are neatly arranged below the photo, maintaining a clean and professional appearance.	The card includes a holographic overlay of the state seal and the Wyoming state flag, which shimmer when viewed from different angles. Fine microprinting of the state name and a repeating pattern of cowboy motifs enhance security. UV-sensitive elements, such as hidden images of the state's natural

		landmarks and additional state symbols, are embedded within the card and become visible under ultraviolet light, providing an extra layer of protection against counterfeiting.

Each state's ID card is meticulously designed to reflect its unique heritage and environment while incorporating advanced security features to prevent forgery and ensure authenticity. The use of holographic overlays, microprinting, and UV-sensitive elements is consistent across all states, although the specific designs and patterns vary to represent each state's distinct identity. These variations not only make each ID visually unique but also enhance the ability of verification personnel to quickly and accurately identify legitimate IDs.

For instance, while California's ID prominently features the Golden Gate Bridge and a multicolored hologram, Texas's ID showcases the state capitol building and longhorn cattle motifs, each serving as a visual cue for authenticity. Similarly, states like New York and Pennsylvania incorporate historical landmarks such as the Statue of Liberty and the Liberty Bell, respectively, into their ID designs, aligning with their rich historical backgrounds.

The integration of UV-sensitive features across all state IDs provides an additional layer of security that is not immediately visible under normal lighting conditions, making it difficult for counterfeiters to replicate these elements without specialized equipment. This, combined with microprinting and holographic overlays, creates a robust defense against ID fraud.

Moreover, the placement and prominence of personal information, such as the cardholder's photograph and state name, are carefully considered to balance aesthetic appeal with functional clarity. This ensures that verification personnel can easily locate and verify essential information without confusion, even when dealing with a high volume of ID checks.

Understanding these state-specific variations is crucial for anyone involved in ID verification processes. Familiarity with the distinct features of each state's ID card enhances the ability to detect inconsistencies and potential forgeries, thereby maintaining the integrity and security of identification systems across the United States. As discussed in previous sections, the combination of traditional security features with modern advancements like digital and mobile IDs continues to evolve, but the foundational elements of design and security remain central to effective ID verification.

The detailed examination of state-specific ID formats underscores the importance of recognizing both common and unique features across all state-issued identification cards. This comprehensive understanding not only aids in accurate and efficient ID verification but also contributes to the broader goal of preventing identity fraud and ensuring the reliability of identification systems nationwide. As technology and security measures continue to advance, staying informed about these variations will remain essential for maintaining robust and secure ID verification practices.

CHAPTER 5

STATE-SPECIFIC ID CHARACTERISTICS

INTRODUCTION TO STATE-SPECIFIC DESIGN ELEMENTS

State-specific design elements on identification cards are a critical component in verifying IDs, ensuring both accuracy and legality. Understanding these design elements can help prevent identity theft, underage alcohol consumption, and the use of fraudulent documents. The unique features that each state incorporates into its ID cards play a crucial role in the authentication process. From color schemes to fonts and background patterns, every detail is a layer of security that provides insight into the authenticity of the card.

Every state in the U.S. takes responsibility for designing its own official identification cards. This makes sense because IDs reflect the legal and cultural norms of their jurisdiction, which may vary from state to state. While all states must comply with certain federal guidelines, there remains a significant amount of flexibility in how these guidelines are met. This variation is a direct result of each state's need to maintain individuality and security, while still aligning with national standards. In fact, some of these differences stem from specific historical or regional trends, as well as legal requirements unique to each state.

For instance, one state's ID may heavily incorporate natural landscapes into its design, reflecting its geographical uniqueness, while another state's design may emphasize historical landmarks or symbols that are meaningful to its local identity. These seemingly aesthetic choices are much more than artistic embellishments; they are deliberate security features that make duplication or alteration difficult. For example, an ID from Colorado might include subtle images of the Rocky Mountains, embedded in layers of security printing, while New York IDs may contain background details representing the Statue of Liberty.

Furthermore, color palettes differ significantly. Some states use light and neutral colors, while others prefer bold and contrasting hues. The choice of colors is often designed to work in tandem with other security features such as UV printing, holograms, and embedded microtext. Bright colors might fade into a hidden message under UV light, while darker shades might reveal tamper-evident security marks when viewed under certain conditions. These details, subtle to the untrained eye, serve a dual purpose: they enhance the visual appeal of the card while complicating attempts at counterfeiting.

Another notable design element is the choice of fonts and typeface. States often employ custom fonts that are not commercially available, making it harder for counterfeiters to replicate official documents accurately. Moreover, the positioning of the text—whether it be the cardholder's name, birthdate, or address—follows a distinct pattern that is consistent for that state. This consistency becomes a powerful tool in identifying irregularities during the verification process. If a font appears off or text alignment seems inconsistent, it is a clear indicator that the ID may be fraudulent.

Security features such as microprinting, holograms, and watermarks are embedded within the design and are unique to each state. For example, microprinting—tiny, detailed text that appears as a line to the naked eye—is often used along the borders of the ID or within specific design elements, such as the state seal. This text is difficult to replicate without the proper technology and is nearly invisible unless viewed with magnification. Many states will also incorporate holographic images that change or shift when the card is tilted. These images often depict state-specific symbols like state birds, flowers, or mottos. Holograms are especially effective in ID verification because they are nearly impossible to replicate with standard printing technologies, adding a robust layer of security.

The choice of materials used to manufacture state IDs is also an essential element of the overall design. Many states have transitioned from simple plastic cards to more advanced polycarbonate materials, which offer enhanced durability and resistance to tampering. Polycarbonate IDs are harder to alter without leaving visible signs of damage, such as cracks or warping. This makes it increasingly difficult for counterfeiters to alter information or swap out photographs on the card without detection. Additionally, the layering techniques used in polycarbonate cards enable states to incorporate security features like ghost images, which are faint, transparent reproductions of the cardholder's photo that are embedded beneath the top layer of the ID.

In addition to visual and material features, states are also increasingly using advanced digital techniques to protect the integrity of their IDs. This includes the use of barcodes and magnetic strips, which store encoded information such as the cardholder's name, address, and date of birth. This information can be scanned and verified electronically, ensuring that the data on the card matches the information stored in state databases. In recent years, many states have also incorporated QR codes or similar elements into their designs, allowing for rapid and secure verification through mobile devices or other digital means. These codes often contain additional layers of encrypted information that can be scanned by law enforcement officers or other authorized personnel, further complicating efforts at fraud.

While we have already discussed the broader importance of secure design features in a previous section, focusing here on state-specific variations illuminates the importance of being familiar with each state's particular methods. In earlier sections about ID validation techniques, we examined the critical role of UV light and magnification tools in detecting counterfeit features. Here, we can extend that understanding by recognizing how the intricate details on state IDs contribute to the same goal. For example, if an ID is designed with intricate microtext along its border, as is the case with many northeastern states, using the proper tools to verify these details ensures a greater likelihood of identifying authentic IDs.

Another layer of complexity is introduced when considering how often states update or redesign their IDs. Some states update their design every few years to incorporate the latest security technologies, while others may go decades without a significant overhaul. As a result, an individual checking IDs must be aware not only of the current design elements but also of any previous designs that might still be in circulation. This is particularly true in states where older adults may still possess legacy IDs that are valid but look significantly different from the most recent versions. These design updates are not just cosmetic; they often include new security features that were not available at the time of the original design. Therefore, staying informed about the timing and scope of state ID redesigns is a crucial part of effective verification.

Despite the diversity in design approaches, there are also some consistencies across state IDs that help maintain a baseline level of familiarity. As noted in previous sections about the Real ID Act, all state IDs must now meet certain federal standards regarding the placement of key information such as full legal names, dates of birth, and signature lines. This consistency allows for some level of predictability when verifying IDs, as these elements will be uniformly located across all state designs. However, even within these federally mandated guidelines, states have room to personalize their layouts and integrate additional security features unique to their own designs.

State-specific design elements are not just a reflection of local pride or individuality; they are an essential part of ID security. Each state balances the need for visually appealing designs with the equally important requirement of fraud prevention. From custom fonts and intricate holograms to advanced materials and digital technologies, every element plays a critical role in ensuring that state IDs remain secure and difficult to counterfeit. Familiarizing oneself with these state-specific details is not just helpful but necessary for anyone involved in ID verification, as these small but crucial design differences often provide the clearest indicators of authenticity.

USE OF COLOR, FONTS, AND HOLOGRAMS

The use of color, fonts, and holograms in state-issued identification cards is fundamental to their design, playing an integral role in preventing fraud and verifying authenticity. These visual elements, though they may appear straightforward to the untrained eye, are actually sophisticated layers of security. Each component is chosen with care to ensure that IDs remain difficult to counterfeit, while also making them easily identifiable for law enforcement officers, bartenders, cashiers, and others who need to verify an ID's legitimacy in everyday interactions.

Color serves as one of the most immediately recognizable elements in an ID's design. Each state has the flexibility to select color schemes that are distinct and reflective of its own character, while still adhering to national standards of legibility and security. Colors are not randomly selected but are carefully chosen to work in conjunction with other features like UV printing and holographic images. For example, certain states may use soft pastel backgrounds, which can be layered with security elements such as fine lines or microprinting. Under normal light, these colors contribute to the aesthetic appeal of the card, but under ultraviolet light, they may reveal hidden patterns or information critical to verification. Other states may favor bold, contrasting colors like deep blues or vivid reds, which are not only visually striking but can also serve as another layer of security by reacting differently when exposed to various light conditions.

Beyond their function as design elements, colors are also often employed to quickly convey information about the ID holder. For instance, different background colors may be used to signify whether the individual is underage or of legal drinking age, a system that allows for swift identification in situations where time is critical, such as at a bar or when purchasing age-restricted items. These age-related color codes are often reinforced with other security features, ensuring that simply altering the color on a counterfeit ID would not be enough to fool trained personnel. Moreover, the interaction between color and other features such as UV ink or holograms can create unique visual effects that would be difficult to replicate with standard printing techniques. This helps in distinguishing between genuine and fraudulent IDs, especially when examined under special lighting.

Fonts, another critical element of ID design, are often overlooked by the casual observer but are, in fact, a significant component of an ID's security framework. States commonly use custom-designed fonts or proprietary typefaces that are not available to the general public, making it difficult for counterfeiters to mimic official IDs with ordinary font libraries. These custom fonts may be subtly different from standard fonts, yet these differences are easily detectable by those familiar with state-issued IDs. In previous sections, we discussed the importance of consistency in state-specific design elements, and the choice of font plays into this consistency by ensuring that key information like the cardholder's name, address, and date of birth is always presented in a uniform manner.

The precise alignment and spacing of text on an ID are also essential factors in its security design. If text appears misaligned, unevenly spaced, or otherwise inconsistent with state standards, it can raise red flags during the verification process. For example, many states use a specific layout for names and dates of birth that follows a predetermined grid. Any deviation from this layout could indicate tampering or counterfeiting. Moreover, fonts used for secondary information, such as organ donor status or license restrictions, are often smaller and more intricately detailed, adding another layer of complexity that would be challenging for forgers to replicate accurately.

While colors and fonts establish the foundation of an ID's design, holograms represent an additional and advanced layer of security that protects against fraud. Holograms are three-dimensional images embedded into the surface of the card, often depicting state-specific symbols, seals, or images that shift when viewed from different angles. These images are not merely decorative but are purposefully included because they are nearly impossible to duplicate with standard printing technologies. The dynamic nature of holograms—changing appearance based on the angle and lighting—makes them a particularly effective deterrent against counterfeiters.

Each state incorporates holograms in its own unique way, often aligning them with other elements of the ID's design. In some states, the hologram may take the form of the state's official seal, which floats across the card when it is tilted. Other states may use more intricate holographic patterns, including symbols like state birds or historical landmarks that are significant to the region. These images serve as a quick visual cue for those verifying the ID, and their complexity ensures that only a genuine card can exhibit these shifting visual effects.

In addition to their visible features, holograms also play a role in enhancing the durability of state-issued IDs. The process used to embed holograms into an ID involves bonding them to the card's surface in a way that resists tampering. If someone attempts to alter or peel off a hologram, the card will show clear signs of damage, which serves as another indication of fraud. This aspect of holographic technology complements the use of polycarbonate materials, discussed in a previous section, which also contribute to the ID's physical integrity and make it more resistant to tampering and alteration.

The placement of holograms on an ID is also highly strategic. Typically, holograms are located in areas of the card where they overlap with key information, such as the cardholder's photograph or signature. This layering ensures that if the card is tampered with—such as by attempting to replace the photo—the hologram will be disturbed, making it evident that the ID is no longer valid. States may also embed micro-holograms, which are tiny holographic elements that are nearly invisible to the naked eye but can be observed under magnification. These micro-holograms often contain repeating patterns or text that adds yet another level of security to the ID.

While these individual elements—color, fonts, and holograms—each contribute to an ID's security, it is their integration and interaction that provide the most robust defense against fraud. For example, the color of the ID may interact with a hologram to create a unique visual effect under different lighting conditions. A trained verifier can recognize these subtleties, distinguishing between an authentic ID and one that may have been altered. Similarly, the fonts used for text may overlap with holographic images, further complicating efforts to alter critical information like names or dates of birth.

In earlier sections about state-specific design features, we explored how different regions incorporate local symbols into their ID designs to both personalize the card and strengthen its security. The use of holograms continues this trend, as many states choose holographic images that are deeply tied to their identity. Whether it's a famous landmark, a state animal, or a motto, these images not only make the card visually unique but also serve as a practical tool in the verification process.

Overall, the thoughtful and deliberate use of color, fonts, and holograms on state-issued IDs creates a multi-layered defense against fraud. By incorporating custom fonts that cannot be easily replicated, unique color schemes that react differently under UV light, and holograms that shift and change depending on the angle, states ensure that their IDs are both functional and secure. These features, when viewed together, provide a level of complexity that deters counterfeiters and gives confidence to those responsible for verifying the authenticity of an ID. Understanding these intricate design choices is essential for anyone involved in ID verification, as even the smallest details can indicate whether a document is genuine or fraudulent.

POSITIONING OF KEY INFORMATION (NAME, DATE OF BIRTH, EXPIRATION DATE)

Here is the detailed state-by-state breakdown of the positioning of key information on identification cards for the states you requested, organized by ID type.

Disclaimer:

This information reflects the current design layouts of state-issued ID cards and driver's licenses. Since these designs may change over time, it is recommended to check with the relevant state's Department of Motor Vehicles (DMV) for the most current version of the ID or driver's license at the time of reference.

Alabama

ID Type	Name Position	Date of Birth Position	Expiration Date Position	Other Information
Driver's License	Top center, under "Alabama" header	Center-left, below the name	Bottom-right, below "EXP" label	Photo on the left. License number is in the top-right. Endorsements at the bottom middle. Address located below the photo.
Identification Card	Top center, under "Alabama" header	Center-left, below the name	Bottom-right, below "EXP" label	Same layout as the driver's license without driving-related endorsements. Signature below the photo.

Alaska

ID Type	Name Position	Date of Birth Position	Expiration Date Position	Other Information
Driver's License	Top left, below the state name	Middle left, under "DOB" label	Bottom right, under "EXP" label	Photo on the left. License number is centered near the top. Signature and restrictions near the bottom center.

| Identification Card | Top left, below the state name | Middle left, under "DOB" label | Bottom right, under "EXP" label | Same layout as the driver's license. No driving restrictions or endorsements. |

Arizona

ID Type	Name Position	Date of Birth Position	Expiration Date Position	Other Information
Driver's License	Top center, below "Arizona" header	Middle left, under "DOB" label	Bottom right, below "EXP" label	Photo on the right. License number is at the top left. Signature below the name. Endorsements and restrictions near the bottom right.
Identification Card	Top center, below "Arizona" header	Middle left, under "DOB" label	Bottom right, below "EXP" label	Same layout as the driver's license but without driving-related data. Signature below the name.

Arkansas

ID Type	Name Position	Date of Birth Position	Expiration Date Position	Other Information

Driver's License	Upper center, below the state name	Middle left, under "DOB"	Bottom right, below the expiration label	Photo on the left. License number at the top right. Signature below the photo. Endorsements at the bottom center.
Identification Card	Upper center, below the state name	Middle left, under "DOB"	Bottom right, below the expiration label	Same layout as the driver's license. No driving restrictions or endorsements.

California

ID Type	Name Position	Date of Birth Position	Expiration Date Position	Other Information
Driver's License	Top left, under "California" header	Middle left, under "DOB" label	Bottom center, under the "EXP" label	Photo on the left. License number at top right. Signature is located below the photo. Class and endorsements are near the bottom center.
Identification Card	Top left, below "California" header	Middle left, under "DOB" label	Bottom center, below the "EXP" label	Same as driver's license but without driving-

				related endorsements .

Colorado

ID Type	Name Position	Date of Birth Position	Expiration Date Position	Other Information
Driver's License	Top right, just under the state name	Middle left, under "DOB" label	Bottom right, below the "EXP" label	Photo on the left. License number is at the top center. Restrictions and endorsements are near the bottom.
Identification Card	Top right, just under the state name	Middle left, under "DOB" label	Bottom right, below the "EXP" label	Similar to driver's license but without endorsements and restrictions.

Connecticut

ID Type	Name Position	Date of Birth Position	Expiration Date Position	Other Information
Driver's License	Upper center, below the state name	Center-left, below the name	Bottom right, below "EXP" label	Photo on the left. License number at the top-right. Signature and class are at the bottom.

| Identification Card | Upper center, below the state name | Center-left, below the name | Bottom right, below "EXP" label | Same layout as the driver's license but without endorsements. Signature below the name. |

Delaware

ID Type	Name Position	Date of Birth Position	Expiration Date Position	Other Information
Driver's License	Top left, under "Delaware" header	Center-left, below the name	Bottom right, under "EXP" label	Photo on the left. License number is at the top center. Endorsements and restrictions are near the bottom.
Identification Card	Top left, under "Delaware" header	Center-left, below the name	Bottom right, under "EXP" label	Similar to the driver's license, but without endorsements or restrictions.

Florida

ID Type	Name Position	Date of Birth Position	Expiration Date Position	Other Information
Driver's License	Upper right, above	Middle left, under	Bottom right, under the	Photo on the right. License number at the top left.

	the photo	"DOB" label	"Expiration Date" label	Signature is below the name. Endorsements near the bottom.
Identification Card	Upper right, above the photo	Middle left, under "DOB" label	Bottom right, under the "Expiration Date" label	Similar to the driver's license. No driving-related data.

Georgia

ID Type	Name Position	Date of Birth Position	Expiration Date Position	Other Information
Driver's License	Top center, under the state name	Middle left, under the name	Bottom right, under the expiration date label	Photo on the left. License number is at the top right. Signature below the photo. Endorsements near the bottom center.
Identification Card	Top center, under the state name	Middle left, under the name	Bottom right, under the expiration date label	Same layout as the driver's license without driving endorsements.

Hawaii

ID Type	Name Position	Date of Birth Position	Expiration Date Position	Other Information
Driver's License	Upper center, under the	Center left,	Bottom right, under the	Photo on the right. License number at the

	state name	below the name	expiration date	top left. Signature at the bottom center.
Identification Card	Upper center, under the state name	Center left, below the name	Bottom right, under the expiration date	Same layout as the driver's license without driving-related endorsements.

Idaho

ID Type	Name Position	Date of Birth Position	Expiration Date Position	Other Information
Driver's License	Top left, under "Idaho" header	Center left, below the name	Bottom right, under "EXP" label	Photo on the left. License number at the top center. Endorsements and restrictions near the bottom.
Identification Card	Top left, under "Idaho" header	Center left, below the name	Bottom right, under "EXP" label	Similar to the driver's license without endorsements or restrictions.

Illinois

ID Type	Name Position	Date of Birth Position	Expiration Date Position	Other Information
Driver's License	Top left, under "Illinois" header	Middle left, under the name	Bottom right, below "EXP" label	Photo on the left. License number is below the state header. Signature is

				below the photo. Class and endorsements near the bottom.
Identification Card	Top left, under "Illinois" header	Middle left, under the name	Bottom right, below "EXP" label	Same layout as the driver's license, but without driving-related endorsements.

Indiana

ID Type	Name Position	Date of Birth Position	Expiration Date Position	Other Information
Driver's License	Top center, under the state name	Center-left, below the name	Bottom right, under "EXP" label	Photo on the left. License number is at the top-right. Signature below the name. Class and endorsements are near the bottom.
Identification Card	Top center, under the state name	Center-left, below the name	Bottom right, under "EXP" label	Same layout as the driver's license without driving-related endorsements.

Iowa

ID Type	Name Position	Date of Birth Position	Expiration Date Position	Other Information

Driver's License	Top left, under "Iowa" header	Middle left, under the name	Bottom right, under the "EXP" label	Photo on the left. License number is at the top center. Signature is below the name. Endorsements are listed near the bottom.
Identification Card	Top left, under "Iowa" header	Middle left, under the name	Bottom right, under the "EXP" label	Same layout as the driver's license. No driving endorsements.

Kansas

ID Type	Name Position	Date of Birth Position	Expiration Date Position	Other Information
Driver's License	Top center, under the state name	Middle left, below the name	Bottom right, below "EXP" label	Photo on the left. License number at the top right. Signature is at the bottom middle. Endorsements and restrictions near the bottom.
Identification Card	Top center, under the state name	Middle left, below the name	Bottom right, below "EXP" label	Same layout as the driver's license without endorsements.

Kentucky

ID Type	Name Position	Date of Birth Position	Expiration Date Position	Other Information
Driver's License	Top left, under "Kentucky" header	Center-left, under the name	Bottom right, below the "EXP" label	Photo on the right. License number is centered at the top. Signature and endorsements near the bottom.
Identification Card	Top left, under "Kentucky" header	Center-left, under the name	Bottom right, below the "EXP" label	Same layout as the driver's license but without endorsements or restrictions.

Louisiana

ID Type	Name Position	Date of Birth Position	Expiration Date Position	Other Information
Driver's License	Top left, under "Louisiana" header	Center-left, under the name	Bottom right, under "EXP" label	Photo on the left. License number is at the top right. Signature is at the bottom middle. Class and endorsements

				are near the bottom.
Identification Card	Top left, under "Louisiana" header	Center-left, under the name	Bottom right, under "EXP" label	Similar to the driver's license but without endorsements.

Maine

ID Type	Name Position	Date of Birth Position	Expiration Date Position	Other Information
Driver's License	Top left, below the state name	Middle left, below the name	Bottom right, under the expiration date	Photo on the right. License number is at the top center. Signature is below the name. Endorsements and restrictions near the bottom.
Identification Card	Top left, below the state name	Middle left, below the name	Bottom right, under the expiration date	Same layout as the driver's license without driving-related data.

Maryland

ID Type	Name Position	Date of Birth Position	Expiration Date Position	Other Information
Driver's License	Upper left, below "Maryland" header	Middle left, under	Bottom right, under "EXP" label	Photo on the left. License number is at the top center. Signature and

		the name		endorsements are near the bottom.
Identification Card	Upper left, below "Maryland" header	Middle left, under the name	Bottom right, under "EXP" label	Same layout as the driver's license but without endorsements.

Massachusetts

ID Type	Name Position	Date of Birth Position	Expiration Date Position	Other Information
Driver's License	Top left, under "Massachusetts" header	Middle left, under the name	Bottom right, below "EXP" label	Photo on the right. License number is at the top left. Signature and endorsements are near the bottom.
Identification Card	Top left, under "Massachusetts" header	Middle left, under the name	Bottom right, below "EXP" label	Same layout as the driver's license but without endorsements.

Michigan

ID Type	Name Position	Date of Birth Position	Expiration Date Position	Other Information
Driver's License	Upper center, below the state name	Middle left, below the name	Bottom right, under "EXP" label	Photo on the left. License number is at the top center. Signature is below the photo. Endorsements and restrictions are near the bottom.
Identification Card	Upper center, below the state name	Middle left, below the name	Bottom right, under "EXP" label	Same layout as the driver's license without driving-related data.

Minnesota

ID Type	Name Position	Date of Birth Position	Expiration Date Position	Other Information
Driver's License	Top left, under "Minnesota" header	Middle left, under the name	Bottom right, under "EXP" label	Photo on the left. License number is at the top right. Signature below the name. Endorsements near the

				bottom center.
Identificatio n Card	Top left, under "Minnesota" header	Middle left, under the name	Bottom right, under "EXP" label	Same layout as the driver's license but without endorsements.

Mississippi

ID Type	Name Position	Date of Birth Position	Expiration Date Position	Other Information
Driver's License	Top left, under the state name	Middle left, below the name	Bottom right, under "EXP" label	Photo on the left. License number is at the top center. Signature below the photo. Endorsements near the bottom center.
Identification Card	Top left, under the state name	Middle left, below the name	Bottom right, under "EXP" label	Same layout as the driver's license but without endorsements.

Missouri

ID Type	Name Position	Date of Birth Position	Expiration Date Position	Other Information
Driver's License	Top left, under	Center-left, under	Bottom right, under	Photo on the left. License number at the top right.

	"Missouri" header	the name	"EXP" label	Signature below the photo. Endorsements near the bottom.
Identification Card	Top left, under "Missouri" header	Center-left, under the name	Bottom right, under "EXP" label	Same layout as driver's license but without endorsements.

Montana

ID Type	Name Position	Date of Birth Position	Expiration Date Position	Other Information
Driver's License	Top center, under the state name	Center-left, below the name	Bottom right, under the "EXP" label	Photo on the right. License number is at the top left. Signature below the name. Endorsements and restrictions near the bottom.
Identification Card	Top center, under the state name	Center-left, below the name	Bottom right, under the "EXP" label	Same layout as driver's license but without endorsements.

Nebraska

ID Type	Name Position	Date of Birth Position	Expiration Date Position	Other Information

| **Driver's License** | Top left, under "Nebraska" header | Center-left, below the name | Bottom right, under the "EXP" label | Photo on the right. License number is at the top left. Signature is below the photo. Class and endorsements are near the bottom. |
| **Identification Card** | Top left, under "Nebraska" header | Center-left, below the name | Bottom right, under the "EXP" label | Same layout as driver's license but without endorsements. |

Nevada

ID Type	Name Position	Date of Birth Position	Expiration Date Position	Other Information
Driver's License	Upper center, below the state name	Center-left, under the name	Bottom right, under the expiration date	Photo on the left. License number is at the top right. Signature below the name. Class and endorsements near the bottom.
Identification Card	Upper center, below the state name	Center-left, under the name	Bottom right, under the expiration date	Same layout as driver's license but without endorsements.

New Hampshire

ID Type	Name Position	Date of Birth Position	Expiration Date Position	Other Information
Driver's License	Top left, under the state name	Center-left, under the name	Bottom right, under "EXP" label	Photo on the right. License number is at the top center. Signature and endorsements near the bottom.
Identification Card	Top left, under the state name	Center-left, under the name	Bottom right, under "EXP" label	Similar layout as driver's license but without endorsements.

New Jersey

ID Type	Name Position	Date of Birth Position	Expiration Date Position	Other Information
Driver's License	Upper center, below "New Jersey" header	Middle left, under the name	Bottom right, under the "EXP" label	Photo on the left. License number is at the top center. Signature and class are near the bottom.
Identification Card	Upper center, below "New Jersey" header	Middle left, under the name	Bottom right, under the "EXP" label	Similar layout as driver's license but without driving endorsements.

New Mexico

ID Type	Name Position	Date of Birth Position	Expiration Date Position	Other Information
Driver's License	Top left, under the state name	Center-left, below the name	Bottom right, under "EXP" label	Photo on the right. License number at the top left. Signature is below the name. Endorsements and restrictions near the bottom.
Identification Card	Top left, under the state name	Center-left, below the name	Bottom right, under "EXP" label	Similar layout as driver's license but without endorsements.

New York

ID Type	Name Position	Date of Birth Position	Expiration Date Position	Other Information
Driver's License	Top left, below the state name	Center-left, under the name	Bottom right, under "EXP" label	Photo on the right. License number at the top center. Signature is below the name. Endorsements are near the bottom.
Identification Card	Top left, below the state name	Center-left, under the name	Bottom right, under "EXP" label	Similar layout as driver's license but without driving endorsements.

North Carolina

ID Type	Name Position	Date of Birth Position	Expiration Date Position	Other Information
Driver's License	Top left, under the state name	Center-left, below the name	Bottom right, under "EXP" label	Photo on the left. License number at the top center. Signature is below the name. Endorsements are near the bottom center.
Identification Card	Top left, under the state name	Center-left, below the name	Bottom right, under "EXP" label	Same layout as driver's license but without endorsements.

North Dakota

ID Type	Name Position	Date of Birth Position	Expiration Date Position	Other Information
Driver's License	Top left, under the state name	Center-left, below the name	Bottom right, under "EXP" label	Photo on the right. License number is at the top left. Signature and class are near the bottom.
Identification Card	Top left, under the state name	Center-left, below the name	Bottom right, under "EXP" label	Similar layout as driver's license but without endorsements.

Ohio

ID Type	Name Position	Date of Birth Position	Expiration Date Position	Other Information
Driver's License	Top left, under the state name	Middle left, under the name	Bottom right, under the "EXP" label	Photo on the right. License number at the top left. Signature is below the name. Endorsements are near the bottom.
Identification Card	Top left, under the state name	Middle left, under the name	Bottom right, under the "EXP" label	Same layout as driver's license but without endorsements.

Oklahoma

ID Type	Name Position	Date of Birth Position	Expiration Date Position	Other Information
Driver's License	Top left, below the state name	Center-left, below the name	Bottom right, below "EXP" label	Photo on the right. License number is at the top center. Signature and class are near the bottom.
Identification Card	Top left, below the state name	Center-left, below the name	Bottom right, below "EXP" label	Similar layout as driver's license but without endorsements.

Oregon

ID Type	Name Position	Date of Birth Position	Expiration Date Position	Other Information
Driver's License	Top center, below the state name	Center-left, under the name	Bottom right, under "EXP" label	Photo on the right. License number at the top left. Signature is below the photo. Endorsements near the bottom.
Identification Card	Top center, below the state name	Center-left, under the name	Bottom right, under "EXP" label	Same layout as driver's license but without endorsements.

Pennsylvania

ID Type	Name Position	Date of Birth Position	Expiration Date Position	Other Information
Driver's License	Top left, below the state name	Center-left, under the name	Bottom right, under the "EXP" label	Photo on the left. License number at the top center. Signature is below the name. Endorsements near the bottom.
Identification Card	Top left, below the state name	Center-left, under the name	Bottom right, under the "EXP" label	Same layout as driver's license but without endorsements.

Rhode Island

ID Type	Name Position	Date of Birth Position	Expiration Date Position	Other Information
Driver's License	Top center, under the state name	Middle left, under the name	Bottom right, under "EXP" label	Photo on the right. License number is at the top left. Signature is near the bottom. Class and endorsements are listed at the bottom.
Identification Card	Top center, under the state name	Middle left, under the name	Bottom right, under "EXP" label	Same layout as driver's license but without driving endorsements.

South Carolina

ID Type	Name Position	Date of Birth Position	Expiration Date Position	Other Information
Driver's License	Upper left, under the state name	Center-left, below the name	Bottom right, under the "EXP" label	Photo on the right. License number at the top left. Signature is near the bottom. Class and endorsements near the bottom.
Identification Card	Upper left, under	Center-left,	Bottom right, under	Same layout as driver's license

	the state name	below the name	the "EXP" label	but without endorsements.

South Dakota

ID Type	Name Position	Date of Birth Position	Expiration Date Position	Other Information
Driver's License	Top left, under the state name	Center-left, under the name	Bottom right, under the expiration date	Photo on the left. License number is at the top right. Signature and endorsements are near the bottom.
Identification Card	Top left, under the state name	Center-left, under the name	Bottom right, under the expiration date	Same layout as driver's license but without driving-related endorsements.

Tennessee

ID Type	Name Position	Date of Birth Position	Expiration Date Position	Other Information
Driver's License	Top left, below the state name	Middle left, below the name	Bottom right, under the "EXP" label	Photo on the right. License number at the top center. Signature below the photo. Endorsements near the bottom center.

Identification Card	Top left, below the state name	Middle left, below the name	Bottom right, under the "EXP" label	Same layout as driver's license but without driving endorsements.

Texas

ID Type	Name Position	Date of Birth Position	Expiration Date Position	Other Information
Driver's License	Top left, under the state name	Center-left, under the name	Bottom right, under the expiration date	Photo on the left. License number is at the top center. Signature below the name. Class and endorsements are listed near the bottom.
Identification Card	Top left, under the state name	Center-left, under the name	Bottom right, under the expiration date	Same layout as driver's license but without endorsements.

Utah

ID Type	Name Position	Date of Birth Position	Expiration Date Position	Other Information
Driver's License	Top left, under the state name	Center-left, under the name	Bottom right, under "EXP" label	Photo on the right. License number is at the top left. Signature and endorsements

				are near the bottom.
Identification Card	Top left, under the state name	Center-left, under the name	Bottom right, under "EXP" label	Similar layout as driver's license but without driving endorsements.

Vermont

ID Type	Name Position	Date of Birth Position	Expiration Date Position	Other Information
Driver's License	Top left, under the state name	Center-left, below the name	Bottom right, under the expiration date	Photo on the left. License number is at the top right. Signature below the name. Endorsements and restrictions near the bottom.
Identification Card	Top left, under the state name	Center-left, below the name	Bottom right, under the expiration date	Same layout as driver's license but without endorsements.

Virginia

ID Type	Name Position	Date of Birth Position	Expiration Date Position	Other Information
Driver's License	Top center, under	Center-left, below the name	Bottom right, under the	Photo on the left. License number at the top center. Signature is

	the state name		expiration date	below the name. Class and endorsements are near the bottom.
Identification Card	Top center, under the state name	Center-left, below the name	Bottom right, under the expiration date	Same layout as driver's license but without endorsements.

Washington

ID Type	Name Position	Date of Birth Position	Expiration Date Position	Other Information
Driver's License	Top left, below the state name	Center-left, below the name	Bottom right, under the "EXP" label	Photo on the right. License number is at the top center. Signature below the name. Class and endorsements near the bottom.
Identification Card	Top left, below the state name	Center-left, below the name	Bottom right, under the "EXP" label	Same layout as the driver's license, but without driving-related endorsements.

West Virginia

ID Type	Name Position	Date of Birth Position	Expiration Date Position	Other Information

Driver's License	Top left, below the state name	Center-left, below the name	Bottom right, under the "EXP" label	Photo on the right. License number is at the top center. Signature and endorsements near the bottom.
Identification Card	Top left, below the state name	Center-left, below the name	Bottom right, under the "EXP" label	Same layout as driver's license but without driving endorsements.

Wisconsin

ID Type	Name Position	Date of Birth Position	Expiration Date Position	Other Information
Driver's License	Top left, under the state name	Center-left, under the name	Bottom right, under the "EXP" label	Photo on the left. License number is at the top center. Signature below the name. Class and endorsements are listed near the bottom.
Identification Card	Top left, under the state name	Center-left, under the name	Bottom right, under the "EXP" label	Same layout as driver's license but without endorsements.

Wyoming

ID Type	Name Position	Date of Birth Position	Expiration Date Position	Other Information
Driver's License	Top left, under the state name	Center-left, under the name	Bottom right, under the "EXP" label	Photo on the right. License number is at the top left. Signature and endorsements are near the bottom.
Identification Card	Top left, under the state name	Center-left, under the name	Bottom right, under the "EXP" label	Same layout as driver's license but without driving endorsements.

7.

PART 3

Advanced Techniques in ID Verification

CHAPTER 6

SPOTTING FAKE IDS

COMMON FAKE ID FEATURES AND HOW TO SPOT THEM

In today's world, the issue of counterfeit identification (ID) is a growing concern, particularly in environments where the verification of identity plays a critical role in ensuring safety, legality, and trust. Fake IDs are commonly used to bypass age restrictions, such as for purchasing alcohol or gaining access to age-restricted venues, but they can also be part of more severe fraudulent activities like identity theft or illegal immigration. With advances in technology, fake IDs are becoming more sophisticated, which makes detecting them more challenging. However, there are still telltale signs and features that, when carefully inspected, can reveal a counterfeit. This section delves into the most common features of fake IDs and provides a detailed approach on how to identify them.

One of the most notable features of a fake ID is a discrepancy in the quality of the material. Genuine state-issued IDs and driver's licenses are usually produced on durable, tamper-resistant materials, often using polycarbonate or PVC. These materials give the cards a certain level of rigidity and durability, allowing them to withstand wear and tear. On the other hand, fake IDs are frequently printed on cheaper, more flexible materials that are noticeably thinner or less robust. When handling an ID, it's crucial to feel for irregularities in the texture or flexibility. A card that bends too easily or feels flimsy may be a counterfeit. Many states also embed tactile elements into their cards, such as raised text or images. Running a finger across the card and feeling for these elements can provide additional insight into its authenticity.

Another clear giveaway is the appearance and placement of the photograph. Legitimate state IDs adhere to strict regulations regarding photo quality, positioning, and size. Photos should be clear, well-lit, and free from distortions. On fake IDs, however, the photo often appears grainy, blurry, or otherwise poorly produced. The image may also be misaligned, either too far to one side or improperly sized. Counterfeiters may struggle with achieving the same high-quality image printing that official agencies use. If a photo looks like it was sloppily pasted onto the ID or printed with low resolution, this can be a red flag. Additionally, one should check for the subtle integration of the photo into the card's background. Many states now use "ghost images," where a smaller, faint version of the person's photograph is embedded elsewhere on the ID as an additional security measure. These ghost images are difficult to reproduce accurately on counterfeit IDs.

The font and typography on an ID card can also signal authenticity or the lack thereof. Official state-issued IDs use precise fonts, often designed specifically for the issuing body, and the text is laid out in a consistent manner. On fake IDs, text may be misaligned, inconsistently spaced, or may use fonts that are clearly different from those used on genuine cards. The spacing between letters and numbers should be uniform, and the text should never overlap with other design elements unless it's intentional as part of the card's security features. Incorrect spelling, inconsistent font sizes, or distorted characters are all potential indicators of forgery. It's also essential to examine the holograms, watermarks, and microprinting that many states incorporate into their IDs. These are some of the most difficult features for counterfeiters to replicate accurately, and their absence, misplacement, or poor quality is often an immediate giveaway of a fake ID.

A significant point to consider when evaluating an ID is the barcode and magnetic stripe. Modern IDs are typically equipped with barcodes or magnetic strips on the reverse side, which store encoded information about the cardholder. Scanning the barcode or swiping the magnetic strip can reveal whether the information embedded matches the visible details on the card, such as the name, date of birth, and license number. Fake IDs frequently fail this test, as counterfeiters may not be able to program the correct information into the barcode or magnetic stripe. Even if the visual elements of the ID appear genuine, a mismatch in the encoded data should prompt further scrutiny. Some fake IDs will have non-functional barcodes or strips that do not scan at all. Therefore, using a scanning device is one of the most reliable ways to confirm an ID's authenticity.

Lighting can also play a critical role in detecting fake IDs. Many state IDs incorporate ultraviolet (UV) features that are invisible to the naked eye but become visible under a UV or black light. These security features often include state seals, images, or other markings that light up in specific areas of the card. Fake IDs frequently lack these UV features, or if they attempt to include them, they are usually inaccurate or misaligned. When placed under UV light, a fake ID may either show no markings or display distorted or incomplete images. In environments where ID verification is crucial, having access to a UV light scanner can greatly enhance the ability to spot a fake.

Another aspect that may reveal a fake ID is its expiration date and issue date. Genuine IDs have consistent time frames for expiration, depending on the state regulations. For instance, most driver's licenses are valid for a set number of years, usually between four to six, depending on the issuing state. A fake ID might have an expiration date that seems out of alignment with what is typical, such as an unusually long or short validity period. Additionally, counterfeit IDs may list an issue date that doesn't correspond with the holder's age. For example, if an ID shows a person's age as 25 but has an issue date from the previous year, it is a clear sign that the ID is likely fake.

In some cases, counterfeiters attempt to alter legitimate IDs by changing key information, such as the date of birth. This is most often done using methods like photo substitution or document washing, where solvents are used to remove the original information and then new details are reprinted over the blank space. Signs of tampering, such as inconsistencies in the background pattern, fuzzy or uneven print quality, or discoloration, can all indicate that an ID has been altered. In cases where tampering is suspected, holding the card up to a light source can help identify areas where the ink or material appears uneven.

Fake IDs can also be detected by comparing the information against a known valid format. Each state has its own specific layout, format, and design elements. The position of key details, such as the name, address, date of birth, and license number, is typically standardized for each state. If an ID does not follow the expected format, it should raise suspicions. Familiarizing oneself with the design and layout of IDs for the states most commonly encountered in a given region is a highly effective strategy for detecting fake IDs. Cross-referencing with legitimate samples can also help in identifying any anomalies or deviations.

Finally, behavior during the presentation of the ID can be revealing. Individuals presenting fake IDs may exhibit nervousness, avoid eye contact, or rush through the process. They may also provide inconsistent personal information when asked to confirm details on the card. Asking simple questions about the information on the ID, such as confirming the zip code or birth date, can sometimes catch a person off guard if they are using a fake ID. Even if an ID looks convincing, the behavior of the person presenting it should be taken into account as part of the overall verification process.

In summary, while fake IDs are becoming more sophisticated, they still exhibit flaws that, when carefully examined, can give them away. From the material quality to the alignment of photographs, the presence of security features like UV markings, and the accuracy of barcodes and magnetic strips, every detail on an ID card provides clues to its authenticity. Combining these physical checks with behavioral observation and, where possible, technology like barcode scanners or UV lights, significantly increases the likelihood of spotting a fake ID. As with any form of verification, familiarity with state-specific ID designs and consistent scrutiny will help ensure that you remain one step ahead of counterfeiters.

TELLTALE SIGNS OF ALTERATIONS

As a professional or someone who will be dealing with issues involving identity verification, recognizing the telltale signs of alterations on identification documents is paramount for ensuring authenticity. Altered IDs, whether they are state-issued identification cards or driver's licenses, pose significant risks not only to businesses but also to security at large. Knowing what to look for can prevent fraud and maintain the integrity of the identification verification process.

One of the most fundamental aspects of identifying alterations is to examine the overall physical condition of the ID. Authentic IDs are typically produced under strict regulations that ensure they remain durable and resistant to wear. An altered ID often shows signs of excessive wear and tear that might suggest tampering. For instance, look for any frayed edges, unusual folding marks, or signs of having been cut and reattached. These signs can indicate that the document has been altered after its original issuance, which raises immediate red flags. Similarly, the presence of smudges, dirt, or stains that are inconsistent with normal handling can also signal that the ID has been manipulated in some form.

Moreover, focusing on the document's printing quality is crucial. Legitimate IDs are created using sophisticated printing technology, resulting in crisp text and high-resolution images. If you observe blurry text, misaligned graphics, or any signs of pixelation, it may suggest that the ID has been printed or altered using inferior methods. This aspect ties back to previous sections regarding the importance of understanding the specific printing techniques used for authentic state IDs. For instance, many states use holographic images, microprinting, and UV-reactive inks to prevent counterfeiting. If these features appear faded, missing, or poorly rendered, it could signify that the ID has undergone alterations.

Next, the examination of the ID's security features is critical. Each state has distinct security features embedded in their identification cards, which are difficult to replicate. These features include holograms, watermarks, and ghost images that are only visible under specific conditions, such as UV light. Familiarizing oneself with these elements is a vital part of the verification process, as they serve as protective measures against forgery. If you find discrepancies in the expected security features or if they appear to be poorly executed, it strongly indicates that the ID may have been tampered with. For instance, a hologram that does not change color under different angles or an image that fails to align correctly with the other features can point to alterations made after the original issuance of the document.

Another critical area to scrutinize is the photo on the ID. The photograph serves as a primary identifier, and any discrepancies regarding its quality or placement can signify alteration. Authentic IDs typically have a photograph that is properly aligned, clear, and features consistent lighting. If the photo appears pixelated, overly edited, or if there are signs of photoshopping, such as mismatched skin tones or unnatural shadows, this may indicate tampering. It is also worth comparing the photo against the person presenting the ID; a clear mismatch raises significant concerns regarding the validity of the document. Furthermore, the presence of multiple images on an ID can indicate that it has been altered or is a counterfeit.

The information displayed on the ID, such as the name, date of birth, and address, should also be closely examined. Authentic IDs follow specific formatting and spacing rules that are consistent across a state's issued IDs. Any inconsistencies in font size, style, or alignment can point to potential alterations. Moreover, misspellings or incorrect information that does not match with known data or previous versions of the ID can be clear indicators that the document has been tampered with. As previously mentioned, it is essential to understand the specific standards for data presentation in ID documents. Each state has its regulations that dictate how information must appear on IDs; thus, any deviation can raise suspicions.

Additionally, the materials used in the ID construction play a significant role in determining its authenticity. Genuine identification cards are usually made from durable plastic or composite materials that are resistant to bending and tearing. If an ID feels flimsy or appears to be made from paper or inferior materials, it could indicate that the document has been altered or is entirely fake. A well-constructed ID should also have a specific weight and texture that distinguishes it from counterfeit versions. This ties back to earlier sections on the physical characteristics of legitimate IDs, emphasizing the importance of tactile evaluation during verification.

When assessing state ID alterations, the presence of adhesive residues is another crucial factor to consider. Often, alterations may involve peeling layers or applying stickers to modify information. If you observe any sticky residues around the edges or on the surface of the ID, it might indicate that the document has been tampered with. This insight aligns with the previous emphasis on the importance of examining an ID holistically. Taking note of every minute detail can provide significant insights into the authenticity of the document in question.

In addition to these physical signs, one must also consider the context in which the ID is presented. An ID that is provided in an unusual manner or with unusual circumstances can raise questions regarding its authenticity. For instance, if the person presenting the ID appears overly nervous or is unable to provide supporting documentation, this should prompt further investigation. Similarly, if the ID does not match the information given by the individual, such as their story or the details about their identity, it may signal potential fraud. The importance of corroborating information from various sources is a crucial element of ID verification that was previously discussed, reinforcing the need for a thorough investigative approach.

Lastly, technology has also become a valuable tool in identifying alterations. Various software applications and devices can verify the authenticity of identification documents by scanning barcodes, magnetic strips, or embedded chips. These technologies can provide immediate feedback on whether an ID is legitimate and if it has been altered in any way. Incorporating such technology into the verification process enhances the effectiveness of identifying altered IDs. It also serves as a reminder of the previous sections regarding the evolution of ID verification methods, where technology continues to play an essential role in enhancing accuracy and reliability.

Recognizing telltale signs of alterations on identification documents is an intricate process that requires keen observation, knowledge of the specific features of genuine IDs, and the ability to correlate various aspects of the ID with the information presented. By being aware of the physical condition, printing quality, security features, photographic integrity, textual information, material quality, and the context of presentation, one can significantly mitigate the risks associated with fraudulent identification. The interplay of these elements forms a comprehensive approach to ID verification, emphasizing the importance of detail and diligence in identifying potential alterations effectively. Ultimately, understanding these telltale signs is critical for anyone involved in identity verification, ensuring that the integrity of the process is maintained and that fraudulent activities are thwarted.

HIGH-QUALITY FAKE IDS: ADVANCED TACTICS FOR DETECTION

The emergence of high-quality fake IDs poses a significant challenge when verifying IDs, and one that gets more and more dicey as time goes on. This is because as technology continues to advance, counterfeiters are employing increasingly sophisticated methods to create convincing replicas of legitimate identification documents. Consequently, developing advanced tactics for detection becomes paramount for those tasked with verifying IDs. Understanding these tactics is not only essential for security personnel and businesses but also crucial for anyone involved in identity checks to safeguard against fraudulent activities.

The first step in detecting high-quality fake IDs lies in recognizing the inherent differences between authentic and counterfeit documents. High-quality fake IDs often mimic legitimate designs, including color schemes, logos, and layouts. However, closer scrutiny reveals subtle discrepancies that can serve as indicators of fraud. For instance, authentic IDs typically undergo a multi-layered production process, which includes the incorporation of specialized materials and advanced printing techniques. Familiarizing oneself with the specific features of genuine state IDs is critical. For example, many states utilize technologies such as UV ink, microprinting, and laser engraving. By being aware of these features, one can better identify when a document lacks such details or displays them poorly, signaling potential forgery.

One of the most significant aspects of high-quality fake IDs is the printing quality. Counterfeiters often rely on commercial printers or low-cost printing technology, which can produce subpar results compared to state-of-the-art equipment used in the production of legitimate IDs. When inspecting an ID, the clarity of text and images should be examined meticulously. Authentic IDs feature sharp, clean lines with no signs of blurring or pixelation. In contrast, a fake ID may display fuzzy or uneven edges, which could indicate that it was produced without the necessary precision. Moreover, color inconsistencies, such as colors that are overly vibrant or too muted, can further suggest that the ID is not genuine.

Security features are an essential component of ID verification and are often the last line of defense against counterfeiting. High-quality fake IDs may attempt to replicate security features, but they frequently fall short in their execution. An example of this is the holographic overlay found on many legitimate IDs. When viewed from different angles, these holograms should shift colors or display distinct patterns. If the hologram appears flat, lacks movement, or is poorly aligned with the ID's overall design, it may indicate that the ID has been forged. Understanding the specific security features of each state's ID, as discussed in previous sections, provides valuable insight into what to look for during verification.

Moreover, examining the ID under different lighting conditions can reveal hidden features that are not immediately visible. For instance, many legitimate IDs contain UV-reactive elements that only appear when exposed to blacklight. These features can include embedded images or patterns that are integral to the ID's authenticity. If these elements are absent or poorly rendered when the ID is subjected to UV light, this could suggest it is a counterfeit. This method of verification highlights the importance of utilizing technology in detecting fake IDs, a topic discussed earlier in relation to modern identification practices. By incorporating such tools, one can enhance their ability to identify high-quality fakes effectively.

Another important tactic in detecting fake IDs involves assessing the physical characteristics of the document. Authentic IDs are made from durable materials designed to withstand wear and tear. If an ID feels flimsy, appears to be made from paper, or exhibits signs of excessive bending or tearing, it raises immediate suspicions. Additionally, inspecting the edges of the ID is vital. Legitimate IDs typically have smooth, rounded edges, while counterfeit IDs may have rough or uneven edges from being poorly cut. A tactile evaluation can reveal much about the document's authenticity, reinforcing the earlier section on the importance of a comprehensive assessment of identification documents.

When examining the photo on the ID, one should pay close attention to the image quality and alignment. The photograph on a genuine ID is usually well-lit and features appropriate contrast, ensuring the individual's face is clear and recognizable. Conversely, high-quality fake IDs may feature poorly edited images, unnatural lighting, or even mismatched skin tones between the photo and the person presenting the ID. Moreover, if the photo appears to be poorly affixed or shows signs of peeling, it may indicate that the ID has been altered post-issuance. Comparing the photo to the individual presenting the ID is crucial, as discrepancies in appearance can often highlight fraudulent attempts.

The textual information displayed on an ID also warrants thorough scrutiny. High-quality fake IDs often attempt to replicate the formatting and structure of authentic IDs. However, inconsistencies may arise in the font style, size, or spacing between characters. An authentic ID typically follows specific formatting rules, and any deviations from this standard can indicate potential tampering. Moreover, examining the data against known databases or previous versions of the ID can provide additional context, revealing whether the information aligns with recognized standards. This aspect reinforces the need for thorough background checks, as highlighted in earlier sections discussing the importance of data verification.

In addition to these physical assessments, context plays a vital role in verifying the legitimacy of an ID. For example, if an individual presents an ID under suspicious circumstances—such as a late-night transaction or in a high-pressure environment—it may warrant additional scrutiny. The behavior of the person presenting the ID can also offer insights; nervousness or hesitation when asked to verify information can be red flags. This aspect underscores the previous sections on behavioral cues during identity verification, emphasizing that human intuition, when combined with careful observation, can provide valuable insights into the authenticity of identification documents.

Another advanced tactic for detecting high-quality fake IDs involves the use of technology and software designed for verification purposes. Many businesses now utilize systems that scan and analyze the data encoded in magnetic strips or barcodes on IDs. These systems can instantly provide a report on whether the ID is legitimate and alert users to any signs of tampering. The integration of such technology into the verification process can significantly reduce the risk of accepting counterfeit IDs, reinforcing the importance of adopting innovative approaches discussed earlier in the context of modern verification methods.

Moreover, fostering a comprehensive understanding of the local laws and regulations regarding ID issuance can enhance detection efforts. Each state has specific guidelines that dictate the design, security features, and information that should be present on IDs. Familiarizing oneself with these regulations enables one to identify discrepancies that may arise with counterfeit documents. This knowledge forms an essential part of the overall verification process, as previously mentioned, allowing for a more informed approach to identifying high-quality fakes.

Finally, training and ongoing education for those responsible for ID verification are critical components in combating the threat posed by high-quality fake IDs. Regular workshops or training sessions focused on emerging trends in counterfeiting techniques can equip personnel with the tools necessary to stay ahead of counterfeiters. This proactive approach enhances the ability to recognize alterations or forgeries, as highlighted in previous sections regarding the importance of continuous improvement in verification practices.

Detecting high-quality fake IDs requires a multifaceted approach that combines careful observation, technological assistance, and an understanding of legal frameworks. By examining the document's physical characteristics, printing quality, security features, and contextual cues, one can significantly mitigate the risks associated with counterfeit IDs. The interplay of these elements creates a comprehensive strategy for identifying fraudulent attempts, emphasizing the importance of vigilance and ongoing education in the ever-evolving field of identity verification. Through the application of advanced detection tactics, individuals and businesses can fortify their defenses against the growing threat of high-quality fake IDs, ultimately safeguarding the integrity of their operations.

CHAPTER 7

REAL ID ACT COMPLIANCE

WHAT IS THE REAL ID ACT?

The REAL ID Act represents a significant shift in the landscape of identity verification in the United States, focusing on enhancing the security of state-issued identification documents. Enacted in 2005 as a response to the events of September 11, 2001, the legislation was introduced to establish minimum security standards for state-issued driver's licenses and identification cards. Its primary aim is to combat terrorism and improve the overall security of the nation by ensuring that these IDs are reliable and difficult to forge.

At its core, the REAL ID Act requires states to meet specific federal standards in the issuance of driver's licenses and identification cards. These standards include verification of the identity and legal presence of applicants through documents such as birth certificates and Social Security cards. Additionally, states must implement measures to enhance the security features of IDs, such as anti-counterfeiting technologies and data encryption, ensuring that these documents are not easily replicated or altered. This foundational framework is crucial, as it establishes a baseline for what constitutes a secure ID, thereby reducing the risk of identity fraud.

One of the critical components of the REAL ID Act is its emphasis on the importance of data management. States are required to maintain a secure database of all issued IDs and to ensure that this data is accessible to law enforcement agencies. This requirement facilitates improved communication between states and federal agencies, allowing for better tracking and verification of identities. The previous section on the role of technology in ID verification underscores the significance of robust data management systems. By aligning with the REAL ID standards, states can enhance their ability to detect fraudulent IDs and streamline the verification process.

As part of the REAL ID Act, states must also implement security features that enhance the physical security of identification cards. This includes measures such as holograms, barcodes, and other advanced technologies that make IDs more difficult to forge. High-quality counterfeit IDs have become increasingly sophisticated, as previously discussed, making it essential for states to adopt advanced security measures that keep pace with evolving counterfeiting techniques. The integration of such security features is a direct response to the growing need for reliable identification documents that can withstand attempts at forgery.

To ensure compliance with the REAL ID Act, states must undergo a thorough verification process. This process involves submitting documentation to the Department of Homeland Security (DHS) demonstrating that they meet the established standards. Once approved, states must then implement the necessary changes to their ID issuance processes. This compliance framework is critical, as it ensures that all states adhere to the same security standards, fostering a sense of uniformity in the verification of identification across the nation. This uniformity ties back to previous sections discussing the significance of understanding individual state regulations in the context of identity verification.

A notable aspect of the REAL ID Act is its implications for federal identification requirements. In 2016, the DHS announced that starting October 1, 2020, only REAL ID-compliant IDs would be accepted for boarding commercial flights and entering federal facilities. This mandate signifies the importance of the REAL ID Act in everyday life, as individuals must ensure that their state-issued IDs meet the requirements to access essential services and travel. As a result, the act has prompted individuals to become more aware of the need for compliant IDs, enhancing the overall understanding of identification verification.

It is important to note that the REAL ID Act does not mandate the issuance of IDs but rather sets forth minimum standards that states must comply with if they wish their IDs to be accepted for federal purposes. As such, some states have chosen not to implement the REAL ID standards, leading to variations in ID verification processes across the country. This inconsistency can create challenges for individuals who travel or require federal services, emphasizing the need for comprehensive understanding and awareness of the specific regulations in each state. This variance in state compliance has been previously discussed, highlighting the importance of being informed about state-specific ID standards to avoid potential complications.

Furthermore, the REAL ID Act has implications for personal privacy and data security. As states are required to maintain secure databases containing personal information, concerns arise regarding the potential for data breaches or unauthorized access to sensitive information. Ensuring that state databases are equipped with robust security measures is vital in safeguarding citizens' identities. The previous sections surrounding the importance of data management reinforce the need for transparency and security in handling personal information within the framework of the REAL ID Act.

The implementation of the REAL ID Act has not been without controversy. Critics argue that the act imposes burdensome requirements on states and could lead to unnecessary complications in the ID issuance process. Some states have faced challenges in meeting the new standards due to financial constraints or administrative hurdles. Additionally, concerns have been raised about the potential for discrimination in the application process, as individuals who may not possess the necessary documentation could be disproportionately affected. This highlights the importance of understanding the implications of the act on different populations and ensuring that the ID verification process remains accessible and fair.

Moreover, the act has prompted sections about the balance between security and personal freedom. Some individuals view the requirements of the REAL ID Act as an infringement on their privacy rights. This tension between security measures and individual liberties is an ongoing debate, one that echoes in various aspects of government policy and regulation. As highlighted in previous sections about identity verification, it is essential to approach these issues with a nuanced understanding, considering both the need for security and the protection of individual rights.

In response to these challenges, states have been working to implement the REAL ID standards while addressing concerns related to accessibility and privacy. Some states have introduced alternative options for individuals who may not have access to the necessary documentation or who may face challenges in the application process. This flexibility is crucial in fostering an inclusive ID issuance system that accommodates diverse populations while still adhering to the security measures mandated by the REAL ID Act.

In summary, the REAL ID Act represents a pivotal development in the landscape of identity verification in the United States, aimed at enhancing the security of state-issued identification documents. By establishing minimum standards for ID issuance, the act seeks to improve the reliability of identification while combating identity fraud and terrorism. The integration of advanced security features, robust data management, and a compliance framework underscores the significance of the REAL ID Act in modern identity verification practices. As individuals navigate the requirements for compliant IDs, an understanding of the act's implications, potential challenges, and ongoing debates is essential in fostering a comprehensive approach to identification verification that balances security with accessibility and individual rights. Ultimately, the REAL ID Act serves as a foundational element in the ongoing effort to enhance the integrity of identification processes while ensuring that individuals can access essential services and travel with confidence.

REAL ID ACT IMPLEMENTATION ACROSS STATES

The implementation of the REAL ID Act across the United States represents a critical evolution in the security and integrity of identification documents. This act was introduced to set stringent federal standards for state-issued driver's licenses and identification cards in response to the vulnerabilities highlighted by the September 11 attacks. While the overarching goal is to enhance national security, the process of implementing these standards varies significantly from state to state, reflecting a patchwork of compliance and individual state challenges.

At its inception, the REAL ID Act required states to verify the identity and legal presence of applicants, mandating the collection of specific documentation, including proof of citizenship or legal residency, Social Security numbers, and proof of residence. States must also incorporate advanced security features into their IDs to deter counterfeiting, ensuring that each ID produced meets federal specifications. This foundational requirement highlights the importance of maintaining a secure identification system, which has been discussed previously in relation to the growing sophistication of counterfeit IDs.

As states began to navigate the implementation of the REAL ID Act, they encountered various challenges, ranging from budgetary constraints to differing political climates. For instance, states with robust infrastructure and existing secure ID systems faced fewer hurdles in meeting compliance requirements. In contrast, others that lacked these foundational elements struggled to adapt their processes, leading to delays in implementation. This disparity illustrates the importance of assessing each state's unique context when discussing the implementation of the REAL ID Act.

Furthermore, the timeline for compliance has varied considerably among states. Initially, the Department of Homeland Security set a deadline for full implementation by 2017. However, this deadline has been extended multiple times due to the complexities involved. Some states, particularly those with smaller populations, faced significant bureaucratic challenges, leading to slower adaptation. The impact of these delays can be seen in the ongoing sections about the need for states to have compliant IDs for various purposes, including air travel and access to federal facilities. In previous sections, the implications of not possessing a REAL ID-compliant ID have been highlighted, emphasizing the need for individuals to stay informed about their state's compliance status.

As of 2024, most states have made substantial progress toward compliance, with a number of them having fully integrated REAL ID standards into their ID issuance processes. States such as California and Florida have developed comprehensive programs that allow residents to easily obtain REAL ID-compliant IDs, integrating the necessary security measures and documentation requirements. These states have invested in technology and training to ensure their DMV staff is equipped to handle the complexities of the application process, reflecting a proactive approach to compliance. This contrasts with states that have resisted the implementation due to concerns over privacy, data security, and perceived federal overreach, which has resulted in ongoing debates about the balance between security and individual rights.

The significance of a uniform identification system across states cannot be overstated, especially in an increasingly mobile society where residents often travel for work, leisure, or family obligations. Discrepancies in ID standards can create confusion and hinder access to essential services, particularly for individuals who may not possess the necessary documents to meet varying state requirements. Previous sections regarding the importance of data management and technological integration in ID verification emphasize the need for a coherent system that can withstand the complexities of interstate travel and identification.

Moreover, many states have taken proactive measures to educate their residents about the changes associated with the REAL ID Act. Awareness campaigns have been essential in ensuring that individuals understand the requirements for obtaining a compliant ID. These campaigns often include informational websites, outreach programs at local DMVs, and partnerships with community organizations to disseminate accurate information. Educating the public has been crucial, as many individuals may not be aware of the need for a REAL ID-compliant ID for air travel and access to federal buildings, a point emphasized in earlier sections focusing on the everyday implications of the REAL ID Act.

In addition to public education, many states have implemented streamlined processes to facilitate compliance. Online services for applying for and renewing IDs have become more common, allowing residents to submit necessary documentation digitally. This modernization of services aligns with the trends in technology previously discussed, reinforcing the importance of accessibility in the ID verification process. The integration of online platforms not only enhances convenience for residents but also improves the efficiency of ID issuance, reducing the burden on state agencies that must process applications and maintain compliance with federal standards.

However, not all states have embraced these changes with equal enthusiasm. Some have raised concerns about the potential for increased government surveillance and the implications of storing personal data in centralized databases. This has led to legal challenges and legislative efforts to push back against certain aspects of the REAL ID Act. In states with strong privacy advocacy, there has been significant debate regarding the implications of data collection and retention practices mandated by the act. These concerns resonate with broader societal sections about privacy and civil liberties, emphasizing the need for a balanced approach to security that respects individual rights, a theme that recurs throughout the conversation on identity verification.

A notable aspect of the implementation process involves the relationship between state and federal agencies. The Department of Homeland Security plays a crucial role in guiding states toward compliance, providing technical assistance, resources, and periodic reviews to assess each state's progress. States are required to submit documentation proving their compliance, which is then evaluated by the federal government. This collaborative dynamic is essential for maintaining the integrity of the REAL ID system. However, some states have expressed frustration with the federal government's approach, citing delays in feedback or support, which can hinder their ability to move forward efficiently.

Looking forward, the continuing implementation of the REAL ID Act will likely evolve as technology advances and public expectations change.

The emergence of biometric technologies and facial recognition systems presents both opportunities and challenges for state ID systems. While these innovations can enhance security and streamline the verification process, they also raise new questions about privacy and data protection. It is crucial for states to navigate these developments carefully, ensuring that they balance the need for security with the protection of individual rights.

The implementation of the REAL ID Act across states represents a complex interplay of security, technology, public awareness, and regulatory compliance. As states work to meet federal standards, the variations in implementation reflect the unique challenges each state faces. The overarching goal of enhancing national security through reliable identification is vital, yet the process must be approached thoughtfully, considering the implications for individuals and the broader society. By fostering a comprehensive understanding of the REAL ID Act's implementation, individuals can better navigate the requirements for compliant IDs, ensuring they are prepared to access essential services while understanding the evolving landscape of identity verification in the United States. The continued dialogue surrounding privacy, security, and accessibility will shape the future of identification standards and practices, necessitating ongoing education and engagement from both state agencies and the public.

IDENTIFYING REAL ID-COMPLIANT CARDS VS. NON-COMPLIANT IDS

Understanding how to identify REAL ID-compliant cards versus non-compliant IDs is crucial for anyone involved in verifying identification documents. As the REAL ID Act establishes specific requirements for state-issued driver's licenses and identification cards, being able to distinguish between compliant and non-compliant IDs has become increasingly important. The implications of this distinction are particularly pronounced in settings where identification is necessary for air travel, access to federal facilities, or in situations where proof of identity is mandatory.

To begin with, REAL ID-compliant cards are designed with specific security features that differentiate them from non-compliant IDs. One of the most notable identifiers is the presence of a star icon in the upper right corner of the card. This star signifies that the ID meets the federal standards established under the REAL ID Act. It is important to note that not all states may have adopted this design, but the star remains a key visual marker to identify a compliant card. The design and layout of the card itself can also provide clues; compliant IDs often feature enhanced security measures, such as holograms, microprinting, and watermarks. These features are implemented to prevent counterfeiting and to verify authenticity, which ties back to sections about the advanced tactics for detecting counterfeit IDs.

In contrast, non-compliant IDs typically lack these specific features. For instance, they may not have the star icon, and their overall design might lack the security elements found in REAL ID-compliant cards. Additionally, non-compliant IDs may not be accepted for federal purposes, meaning that individuals may encounter difficulties when trying to use them for air travel or entering federal buildings. Recognizing these differences is paramount for businesses and organizations that require reliable identification for their operations.

Another critical factor in identifying REAL ID-compliant cards is the information displayed on the card. Compliant IDs will have full name, date of birth, gender, address, and, importantly, will often include a unique identification number. The inclusion of the cardholder's legal status is also significant. For example, a REAL ID-compliant card will often have a clear indication of the cardholder's citizenship or legal presence in the United States, further reinforcing the ID's legitimacy. Non-compliant IDs may have vague or incomplete information, making them more susceptible to scrutiny.

Moreover, it is essential to examine the material used for the card. REAL ID-compliant cards are typically made from more durable materials than non-compliant IDs, which may be printed on lower-quality plastic or paper. The texture and overall feel of the card can provide clues about its authenticity. As discussed previously, advanced printing techniques and secure materials are part of the measures taken to enhance the security of identification documents, so this aspect should not be overlooked.

While these visual and material characteristics provide a strong basis for differentiating between compliant and non-compliant IDs, the verification process does not end there. Verification methods should also include a check of the card's features under different lighting conditions. Many REAL ID-compliant cards are designed to reveal specific elements, such as watermarks or embedded holograms, when held under UV light. This feature adds an additional layer of security, allowing for real-time verification that can significantly reduce the risk of accepting fraudulent IDs.

In addition to the physical characteristics, a comprehensive approach to identifying compliant cards involves utilizing technological solutions. Various applications and software are available that can scan and analyze IDs, verifying their authenticity against a database of known compliant IDs. This technological approach enhances the verification process by offering immediate feedback about the ID's legitimacy. As previously discussed in relation to the importance of data management, the integration of technology in the ID verification process plays a crucial role in ensuring security and compliance.

It is also important to consider the context in which the ID is being presented. Understanding the common practices and regulations in specific industries can provide further insight into what constitutes a compliant ID. For instance, in the travel industry, employees are trained to recognize the nuances of REAL ID-compliant cards as they relate to boarding passes and security checkpoints. This industry-specific knowledge can help individuals in roles that require ID verification to differentiate between compliant and non-compliant IDs effectively.

Beyond the physical attributes of IDs, the knowledge and training of those responsible for ID verification cannot be overlooked. Ensuring that employees are educated on the specifics of the REAL ID Act and the various state compliance measures is critical for effective identification verification. Training sessions should include practical demonstrations of how to assess IDs, as well as updates on any changes in regulations or design standards. This approach aligns with previous sections about the importance of public education and awareness regarding ID requirements. Empowering individuals with the right knowledge enhances their ability to spot inconsistencies and assess ID authenticity.

It is also essential to remain aware of the potential for counterfeit IDs that mimic REAL ID-compliant cards. As technology advances, counterfeiters are becoming more sophisticated, creating fake IDs that closely resemble compliant cards. Being able to recognize subtle discrepancies in the printing, text, or overall design can make the difference between accepting a legitimate ID and a fraudulent one. Previous sections highlighting advanced tactics for detecting high-quality fake IDs underscore the need for vigilance and thorough verification practices.

Furthermore, there are ongoing updates and changes to the REAL ID requirements that can affect how IDs are issued and verified. Staying informed about the latest developments in ID regulations is crucial for anyone involved in ID verification. For example, state compliance deadlines and updates on federal standards can shift the landscape of what constitutes a compliant ID. Regularly consulting resources and engaging in professional development can equip individuals with the tools necessary to adapt to these changes.

Identifying REAL ID-compliant cards versus non-compliant IDs requires a multifaceted approach that encompasses visual inspection, knowledge of the specific features and materials used in the cards, technological verification methods, and contextual understanding of industry practices. As the landscape of identification continues to evolve, so too must the strategies employed by those tasked with ID verification. By remaining vigilant and informed, individuals can navigate the complexities of identification verification with confidence, ensuring that they uphold the standards set forth by the REAL ID Act while facilitating secure access to essential services. The ability to discern between compliant and non-compliant IDs is not just a technical skill; it is an integral part of maintaining security and integrity in an increasingly mobile and interconnected world.

CHAPTER 8

USE OF ID SCANNERS AND MOBILE APPS

HOW ID SCANNERS WORK

Understanding how ID scanners work is essential for anyone involved in the process of verifying identification documents. These devices play a crucial role in enhancing security measures across various sectors, including transportation, retail, hospitality, and law enforcement. At their core, ID scanners are designed to read and interpret the information embedded within identification documents, ensuring accuracy and reliability in the verification process.

ID scanners typically employ optical character recognition (OCR) technology to capture and analyze the data found on IDs, such as driver's licenses, passports, and state identification cards. When a user presents an ID to an ID scanner, the device utilizes a combination of light sensors and imaging technology to create a digital representation of the document. The scanner shines light on the ID, illuminating the printed text, barcodes, and any embedded security features. This process involves capturing an image of the front and, in some cases, the back of the ID. As discussed in earlier sections about security features on IDs, these scanners are designed to recognize various security elements, which can provide additional layers of verification.

Once the ID is scanned, the OCR technology extracts the textual information displayed on the card. This typically includes the cardholder's name, date of birth, address, and identification number. In addition to basic information, some advanced scanners can read machine-readable zones (MRZs) that are present on passports and other identification documents. These zones often contain encoded data that provide further verification of the ID holder's identity. By processing this information electronically, ID scanners eliminate the potential for human error that can occur during manual checks, a point that ties back to the earlier sections about the importance of accuracy in ID verification.

In addition to OCR, many ID scanners also utilize barcode scanning technology. Most modern identification documents are equipped with barcodes, which encode essential information about the cardholder. When an ID is scanned, the barcode reader decodes this information quickly, providing instant verification. This technology not only speeds up the verification process but also helps ensure that the data being read is consistent with the visible information on the card. If there is a discrepancy between the information extracted through OCR and the data encoded in the barcode, the scanner can alert the user to potential issues.

Moreover, some ID scanners are equipped with sophisticated verification capabilities that extend beyond simple data extraction. For example, many scanners can analyze the card for embedded security features that are not immediately visible. This includes ultraviolet (UV) markings, holograms, and microprinting. When the scanner illuminates the ID, it can detect these features to confirm authenticity. The integration of such technology is particularly relevant given the increasing sophistication of counterfeit IDs, which has been highlighted in previous sections. By cross-referencing the ID's features with a database of known genuine IDs, scanners can provide an additional layer of security against fraud.

A significant advantage of ID scanners is their ability to connect to centralized databases for real-time verification. Many scanners can be linked to state or federal databases, allowing users to check the validity of an ID against official records. This capability is crucial for various applications, such as verifying whether a driver's license is active or if the ID holder has any outstanding warrants. Access to such databases can streamline operations in businesses where identification verification is frequent, enhancing both efficiency and security. This technology aligns with previous sections about data management and the importance of having up-to-date information at one's fingertips.

Another critical aspect of ID scanners is their adaptability to different types of identification documents. While many scanners are optimized for driver's licenses, they can often be adjusted to read other forms of ID, such as military identification cards, passports, or even student IDs. This versatility makes them invaluable tools in environments where multiple forms of identification are presented, ensuring that staff can accurately and efficiently verify a variety of documents. In earlier sections, the section around the need for flexible verification processes is underscored, emphasizing the necessity of having technology that can adapt to various scenarios.

Furthermore, the user interface of ID scanners has evolved significantly to improve usability and accessibility. Many modern scanners feature intuitive touchscreens that guide users through the scanning process, displaying real-time feedback and alerts. This user-friendly design reduces the likelihood of mistakes during verification, which can be particularly beneficial in high-volume environments such as bars, clubs, and airports. Additionally, advanced scanners can store historical data about IDs that have been scanned, allowing businesses to track trends and identify potential issues over time. This feature reflects the ongoing conversation about the role of technology in enhancing security measures.

It is also essential to consider the implications of privacy and data security when using ID scanners. Given that these devices collect sensitive information, it is crucial for organizations to implement appropriate data protection measures. This includes ensuring that the data is encrypted, securely stored, and that users are trained on how to handle sensitive information responsibly. The conversation surrounding privacy concerns resonates with earlier sections regarding the balance between security and individual rights. Businesses must comply with local and federal regulations regarding data collection and usage, fostering trust between the organization and its customers.

In addition to privacy considerations, regular maintenance and updates of ID scanning technology are necessary to ensure optimal performance. As technology evolves, manufacturers frequently release updates to enhance scanning capabilities, address vulnerabilities, and improve user experience. Keeping scanners up-to-date can significantly improve their accuracy and effectiveness, thereby reducing the likelihood of errors in the verification process. This need for ongoing evaluation and adaptation reflects earlier sections about the importance of staying informed and responsive to changes in technology and regulations.

Despite the advanced capabilities of ID scanners, users must still remain vigilant during the verification process. While technology can significantly enhance accuracy, it is not infallible. Training employees to recognize the limitations of ID scanners and the importance of cross-verifying information manually is crucial. This practice ties back to earlier conversations about the need for comprehensive knowledge and training among those responsible for ID verification. Employees should be aware of the nuances of specific identification documents and the potential for sophisticated counterfeits that scanners may struggle to identify.

As businesses and organizations increasingly adopt ID scanning technology, the role of these devices in the broader context of security and compliance cannot be overstated. They serve as critical tools for preventing fraud, verifying identities, and ensuring adherence to legal and regulatory requirements. By enhancing the accuracy and efficiency of ID verification processes, scanners contribute to a safer environment for both businesses and their customers.

Understanding how ID scanners work is vital for anyone involved in identity verification processes. Through the use of optical character recognition, barcode scanning, and real-time database connectivity, these devices provide a comprehensive solution for verifying the authenticity of identification documents. The integration of advanced security features, user-friendly interfaces, and data management capabilities further enhances their utility across various sectors. As technology continues to evolve, it is crucial for organizations to remain informed about advancements in ID scanning and to balance security measures with privacy considerations. By leveraging ID scanners effectively, businesses can improve their operational efficiency while maintaining high standards of security and compliance.

LEGAL CONSIDERATIONS AND LIMITATIONS

When using ID scanners and verification apps, it is essential to understand the legal landscape surrounding these tools, as well as their limitations. ID scanners and apps have become valuable resources for businesses that need to confirm the authenticity of identification documents, whether for age verification, access control, or other regulatory requirements. However, the use of these technologies must always be aligned with both federal and state laws to prevent unintended legal complications and ensure that privacy rights are upheld. Failing to navigate these laws properly can result in costly penalties or legal action, making it imperative to be aware of the responsibilities and boundaries associated with using these tools.

One of the primary legal considerations involves privacy laws, which play a significant role in regulating how personal information contained in identification documents can be collected, stored, and shared. In the United States, various laws at the federal and state levels address privacy concerns. For instance, the federal Driver's Privacy Protection Act (DPPA) restricts the release and use of personal information from state motor vehicle records, which includes details like name, address, and photograph. Businesses using ID scanners must ensure that they do not retain personal data beyond what is legally permissible or necessary. For instance, while it may be acceptable to verify the age of a customer in a bar setting, it may not be lawful to store their information for future use without explicit consent. Consent is a key factor here, and businesses should obtain it in a clear and straightforward manner, with proper documentation of how the information will be used.

In some states, specific laws regulate the retention and sharing of scanned data. California, for instance, has stringent privacy laws under the California Consumer Privacy Act (CCPA), which grants residents the right to know what personal data is being collected, how it is used, and the ability to opt out of having their data sold or stored. This law affects any business that operates in California or serves its residents, regardless of where the business itself is located. Other states, such as Illinois, have biometric data protection laws, like the Illinois Biometric Information Privacy Act (BIPA), that govern how businesses handle biometric information obtained from ID scanning, including fingerprints or facial recognition features. These laws require explicit consent for the collection and use of such data and often come with strict penalties for non-compliance. Businesses need to be mindful of these regulations, as violating them could lead to class-action lawsuits or significant fines, sometimes amounting to thousands of dollars per violation.

Another important legal consideration revolves around the Fair Credit Reporting Act (FCRA), which applies to businesses that may use ID verification tools for employment purposes or background checks. The FCRA requires that businesses obtain explicit consent from individuals before running background checks, including verifying identities. This law also gives individuals the right to dispute incorrect information found during the verification process. In scenarios where ID scanners and verification apps are employed for pre-employment screenings, businesses must ensure that they comply with these obligations, provide necessary disclosures, and follow appropriate steps if an individual wishes to dispute the results of the verification. Non-compliance with the FCRA can result in legal action from the Federal Trade Commission (FTC) or lawsuits from affected individuals.

State laws also play a crucial role in determining how ID scanning and verification tools can be legally used. For example, the legality of scanning IDs may differ depending on the industry. Liquor stores and bars may have broader legal allowances for scanning IDs to verify age, but businesses operating outside of such industries may face stricter restrictions on the collection of personal data. In some states, the use of ID scanners in retail settings may only be permitted if the business can demonstrate that there is a clear need to prevent fraud or theft. Businesses should carefully assess their specific use cases for ID scanning and ensure that they are compliant with local laws that govern their particular industry.

Moreover, the legal limitations of ID scanners and verification apps should not be overlooked. While these tools can be highly effective in verifying the authenticity of government-issued IDs, they are not foolproof. Scanning technologies are not immune to error, and false positives or negatives can occur. Some apps rely on databases that may not be entirely up-to-date, or their systems may be unable to detect high-quality counterfeit IDs. In the previous section on the reliability of ID scanners, we highlighted that verification apps and devices may not catch every instance of fraud, especially when dealing with sophisticated forgeries. Legal limitations arise when businesses mistakenly deny service or access to individuals based on these errors. It is important to recognize that relying solely on technology may not be enough to meet legal or regulatory standards, and manual checks may still be required in certain situations.

Additionally, certain federal laws, like the Americans with Disabilities Act (ADA), may place restrictions on how ID scanners are used in specific contexts. For instance, businesses must ensure that their methods of verification do not discriminate against individuals with disabilities. If ID verification technology creates barriers for individuals with disabilities, such as those who cannot physically present an ID in a traditional format, businesses could face ADA compliance issues. Offering alternative methods of verification for people who cannot use standard identification forms is necessary to remain compliant with these regulations.

The overarching concern of data security also intersects with legal considerations when using ID scanners. Data breaches are a significant risk for businesses that store information obtained from IDs. If a scanner or app collects personal data, there is a legal obligation to protect that data from unauthorized access. A failure to do so can lead to both federal penalties and state-level sanctions under data breach notification laws. For example, many states require businesses to notify customers if their personal information has been compromised in a breach. The legal consequences of a data breach can be severe, including hefty fines and the potential for class-action lawsuits. Companies using ID verification technology should employ robust security measures, such as encryption and regular audits, to protect against data breaches and comply with applicable laws regarding data protection.

Finally, businesses must remain up-to-date with evolving legal standards, as legislation regarding digital privacy and data security continues to evolve rapidly. Laws like the CCPA and GDPR (General Data Protection Regulation) in the European Union have set a precedent for other states and countries to follow. Staying informed about changes in privacy laws, both at the federal and state levels, is essential for businesses that rely on ID verification technology. Ignorance of new or updated laws is not a defense in legal disputes, and businesses are responsible for keeping their practices in line with current legal requirements.

While ID scanners and verification apps provide powerful tools for ensuring compliance with age restrictions, preventing fraud, and safeguarding public safety, they come with a complex web of legal obligations and limitations. Understanding privacy laws, data protection regulations, and the potential legal pitfalls of relying solely on technology is vital for any business that employs these tools. By staying informed, securing consent where necessary, and implementing robust data protection measures, businesses can use ID verification technology responsibly and in compliance with the law.

BEST MOBILE APPS FOR VERIFYING IDS

In today's fast-paced world, the demand for efficient and reliable identification verification has led to the development of numerous mobile applications designed specifically for this purpose. These mobile apps have become indispensable tools for businesses and organizations that require quick, accurate, and secure verification of IDs. As discussed in previous sections regarding the need for accuracy and security in ID checks, leveraging mobile technology can significantly enhance the verification process, making it more efficient and user-friendly.

When choosing the best mobile apps for verifying IDs, several features are crucial to consider. These features include the ability to scan and analyze different types of identification documents, support for various formats such as barcodes and QR codes, real-time database connectivity for instant verification, and user-friendly interfaces that simplify the process for staff. Security features such as data encryption and compliance with privacy laws are also essential, as they protect sensitive personal information from potential breaches.

One notable app in the ID verification space is **IDScan**, which offers comprehensive solutions for businesses needing to verify customer identities. This app utilizes advanced optical character recognition (OCR) technology to read information from government-issued IDs and credit cards. IDScan's capabilities include scanning barcodes, MRZs, and conducting live ID verification through databases. The app also provides real-time alerts for fraudulent or expired IDs, which is vital in high-security environments. Given the importance of keeping accurate records, IDScan allows users to store and manage ID data securely, maintaining compliance with legal requirements while enhancing operational efficiency.

Another leading app is **VeriScan**, known for its simplicity and effectiveness. VeriScan provides a straightforward user interface that makes it easy for staff to navigate the ID verification process. This app supports a wide range of ID types, including driver's licenses, passports, and state identification cards. The app's standout feature is its ability to connect to a cloud database for real-time verification. When an ID is scanned, VeriScan cross-references the information against government databases, ensuring that the ID is valid and not reported as lost or stolen. This capability aligns with earlier sections about the importance of immediate feedback in ID verification, allowing businesses to act quickly in case of discrepancies.

IDChecker is another app gaining traction in the ID verification landscape. This app stands out due to its extensive database of known fraudulent IDs, which helps businesses quickly identify counterfeits. IDChecker utilizes advanced image processing techniques to assess the quality and authenticity of the ID being presented. This is particularly useful for environments such as bars, clubs, and age-restricted venues, where counterfeit IDs are prevalent. As mentioned in previous sections on detecting high-quality fake IDs, having access to a comprehensive database of known fakes is crucial for effective verification.

TrustID is particularly well-suited for businesses operating in regulated industries, such as finance and healthcare. TrustID not only verifies the authenticity of IDs but also checks against various regulatory compliance standards. This feature is critical for organizations that must adhere to strict KYC (Know Your Customer) and AML (Anti-Money

Laundering) regulations. TrustID's integration with existing systems allows for seamless workflows, ensuring that businesses can maintain compliance without sacrificing efficiency. This highlights the need for organizations to select ID verification tools that align with their specific regulatory obligations, as discussed in previous sections.

For those seeking a more versatile and multifunctional solution, **CamScanner** deserves mention. While primarily known as a document scanning app, CamScanner also includes features for scanning and verifying IDs. Users can take pictures of identification documents, which the app then enhances for better readability. While it may not have all the advanced verification capabilities of dedicated ID verification apps, CamScanner is a valuable tool for businesses needing a quick solution without investing in specialized software. This flexibility can be beneficial in environments where occasional ID checks occur, supporting earlier sections about the importance of adaptability in verification processes.

MobileVerify is another app that focuses on ensuring security through advanced biometric features. This app combines ID verification with biometric checks, such as facial recognition. When an ID is scanned, MobileVerify compares the photo on the ID to a live photo taken through the app, ensuring that the individual presenting the ID matches the person it was issued to. This dual-layer verification enhances security, particularly in high-stakes environments such as airports and government facilities, where the risk of identity fraud is heightened. This technology reflects the previous section regarding the increasing role of biometric verification in ID checks.

Moreover, **ID.me** has emerged as a leading app in the realm of online identity verification, especially in the context of digital services. As more businesses transition to online platforms, having a reliable means of verifying identities becomes paramount. ID.me provides a secure online platform for users to verify their identities using various documents, including driver's licenses and social security cards. This app is particularly useful for government agencies and online retailers that need to verify user identities remotely while maintaining stringent security standards. The integration of such digital verification methods is essential for adapting to the changing landscape of commerce and security, aligning with earlier points made about the evolving nature of ID verification.

In addition to these applications, it is crucial to discuss the role of **data privacy** and **security** in the selection and implementation of ID verification apps. Given the sensitive nature of the information being handled, businesses must choose apps that prioritize data protection. Look for applications that comply with relevant privacy laws, such as the General Data Protection Regulation (GDPR) and the California Consumer Privacy Act (CCPA). Moreover, features like end-to-end encryption, secure data storage, and robust access controls are critical in ensuring that personal information remains protected against unauthorized access and breaches. As emphasized in previous sections regarding legal considerations, understanding the implications of data handling is vital for organizations.

Training and familiarizing staff with the chosen ID verification applications is also paramount. Even the most advanced technology will not yield its full potential if the personnel using it do not understand how to operate it effectively. Comprehensive training programs should be implemented to ensure that employees are proficient in using the mobile apps and are aware of the features available for maximizing security and efficiency. This emphasis on staff training connects with earlier sections about the need for ongoing education in the realm of ID verification.

The increasing reliance on mobile applications for ID verification reflects the evolving demands of various industries for efficient, secure, and user-friendly solutions. Apps such as IDScan, VeriScan, IDChecker, TrustID, CamScanner, MobileVerify, and ID.me each bring unique features and advantages, catering to different needs and contexts. Selecting the appropriate app requires consideration of various factors, including the types of IDs being verified, the regulatory environment, and the importance of data privacy and security. Furthermore, integrating training and ongoing education for employees using these tools is essential for ensuring effective and compliant verification practices. By harnessing the capabilities of the best mobile apps for verifying IDs, organizations can enhance their security measures while providing seamless and efficient service to their customers.

CHAPTER 9

BEST PRACTICES FOR ID VERIFICATION IN DIFFERENT INDUSTRIES

RETAIL AND ALCOHOL SALES

In the retail and alcohol sales industries, ID verification is not just a matter of compliance but a crucial element of responsible business practices. The effective use of ID verification techniques helps prevent the sale of age-restricted products to minors, protects businesses from fraud, and ensures adherence to state and federal regulations. The methods and technologies used in verifying IDs must be precise and reliable, especially in these industries where legal consequences can be significant. To properly implement ID verification practices, businesses need to align their processes with legal requirements, employ appropriate technologies, and train staff thoroughly. The dynamics of ID verification can vary based on the nature of the business, and understanding how to adapt these practices within the unique environments of retail and alcohol sales is key to ensuring compliance and preventing potential legal ramifications.

In retail, ID verification is often necessary when a business sells age-restricted products such as tobacco, lottery tickets, or certain medications. State laws typically mandate strict age limits for these products, requiring businesses to verify a customer's age before completing a transaction. The previous section touched on the importance of accurately checking state-issued IDs to confirm an individual's age, a practice that is even more critical in retail environments where failure to do so can result in hefty fines, license revocation, and other legal penalties. This underscores the need for businesses to have consistent, reliable methods for verifying IDs, regardless of whether the transaction is taking place in a physical store or online. For physical retail stores, visual checks of the ID, supported by technological aids such as scanners or verification apps, can help confirm authenticity. The use of ID scanners, which was elaborated upon earlier, can mitigate the risk of human error during manual checks, ensuring that key features like holograms, barcodes, and expiration dates are inspected thoroughly and accurately.

Alcohol sales, whether in a retail setting or a bar, bring even greater scrutiny to ID verification practices. Alcohol is one of the most heavily regulated products in the United States, and the sale of it is subject to both federal and state laws that mandate strict ID verification. Selling alcohol to a minor is a serious offense, with potential legal consequences that can include fines, suspension of liquor licenses, or even the permanent closure of a business. In addition to traditional retail stores that sell alcohol, bars, restaurants, and events where alcohol is served must all maintain rigorous ID verification procedures. As highlighted in earlier sections about the reliability of verification technologies, simply scanning an ID may not always suffice, especially in high-risk environments like bars or clubs where underage individuals may attempt to use fake or altered IDs. The technology must be supported by well-trained staff who can identify potential red flags and handle situations where an ID might not seem authentic.

In both retail and alcohol sales, staff training is a critical component of effective ID verification. Employees who are tasked with checking IDs must be thoroughly educated on the features of various state IDs and the types of government-issued identification that are acceptable. Inconsistencies in training can lead to errors in judgment, such as overlooking signs of tampering or failing to recognize out-of-state IDs. Staff should be trained not only on the technical aspects of scanning an ID but also on the legal requirements specific to the business's location. For instance, in some states, only government-issued IDs are acceptable forms of identification, while in others, foreign passports may also be valid. A key point raised in the section on legal considerations is the importance of knowing which forms of identification are legally acceptable in different jurisdictions, a principle that holds true across both retail and alcohol sales industries.

Another layer of complexity comes into play with online retail, particularly when age-restricted products like alcohol or tobacco are sold through e-commerce platforms. In these cases, businesses must adopt digital solutions that effectively verify the age of the purchaser before shipping the product. Online ID verification tools typically rely on document upload systems, where customers are required to scan and submit a valid form of identification, or on databases that cross-reference customer information to confirm age. However, even with these technological measures in place, there is still the potential for fraud. A person might attempt to use another individual's ID or manipulate the system to bypass verification. As discussed in previous sections, the limitations of technology mean that human oversight remains necessary. Online retailers must therefore implement secondary checks, such as requiring an adult signature upon delivery or utilizing facial recognition technology to compare the person making the purchase with the individual in the ID photo.

In addition to technology and training, businesses must also be vigilant about data privacy concerns, particularly when handling sensitive personal information. ID verification in both retail and alcohol sales often involves collecting and storing personal data such as names, addresses, and birthdates, which are protected under various privacy laws. Earlier sections emphasized the need for businesses to comply with data protection laws like the Driver's Privacy Protection Act (DPPA) and the California Consumer Privacy Act (CCPA), and this becomes especially pertinent in industries where personal data is frequently collected for verification purposes. Businesses must ensure that they have robust security protocols in place to protect customer information from data breaches. This might involve encrypting the data collected during ID verification or limiting access to only those employees who absolutely need it. Failure to safeguard this information could result in significant legal liabilities, including fines and potential lawsuits from customers whose information has been compromised.

One of the common challenges in both retail and alcohol sales is dealing with false identification, whether it be counterfeit IDs or legitimate IDs that have been altered or stolen. Modern technology has made it easier for individuals to produce high-quality fake IDs, and businesses must remain vigilant in spotting them. This is where the integration of ID scanners and mobile verification apps can offer significant value. These tools are designed to recognize the security features embedded in state-issued IDs, such as holograms, watermarks, and microtext, which are difficult to replicate. When businesses combine these technological tools with well-trained employees who understand the nuances of ID verification, they significantly reduce the risk of being duped by a fake ID. Earlier sections on the evolving nature of ID counterfeiting highlight the importance of keeping verification systems up to date, as new methods of fraud emerge over time.

Additionally, businesses in the alcohol sales industry must be prepared to handle situations where customers present alternative forms of ID, such as military IDs or international passports. In these cases, the ID scanning technology used in retail settings might not always be equipped to verify these forms of identification, requiring staff to rely on visual inspections and manual verification methods. Ensuring that employees are familiar with these less common forms of ID, and how to verify them properly, is just as important as understanding how to scan a state driver's license.

Overall, the best practices for ID verification in the retail and alcohol sales industries involve a careful balance of technology, training, and adherence to legal requirements. By staying current with legal standards, using effective technology, and ensuring staff are properly trained, businesses can safeguard themselves from the risks associated with selling age-restricted products. Moreover, these practices not only protect the business from legal consequences but also contribute to broader societal goals of preventing underage consumption of alcohol and tobacco and reducing identity fraud. The complexities of ID verification across different states, which were outlined in previous sections, underscore the importance of maintaining a high level of vigilance and adaptability in these industries, ensuring that businesses remain compliant and secure at all times.

CASINOS AND GAMBLING

Casinos, both physical and online, operate in an industry where the accurate verification of a person's identity is not only necessary for ensuring age restrictions but also for complying with anti-money laundering (AML) regulations and preventing fraud. Given the potential legal and financial consequences of failing to properly verify identities, best practices in this sector must be meticulously followed. This means that casinos must utilize advanced technologies, train their staff rigorously, and continuously stay updated on evolving laws and regulations that govern ID verification.

The first and perhaps most critical aspect of ID verification in casinos is ensuring that all patrons are of legal gambling age. Each state in the U.S. has its own legal age requirements for gambling, with most states setting the minimum age at either 18 or 21 years old, depending on the type of gambling involved. For casinos, ensuring that no one underage accesses the gaming floor or participates in online gambling activities is essential. The legal ramifications of permitting minors to gamble are severe, ranging from fines and penalties to the potential loss of gambling licenses. As discussed earlier, businesses in the alcohol and retail industries must implement robust ID verification systems to ensure compliance with age restrictions, and this necessity is magnified in the gambling industry, where the stakes are significantly higher due to the regulatory environment surrounding casinos.

In the physical casino environment, where foot traffic can be immense, it is vital that ID verification processes are fast, efficient, and foolproof. Typically, casinos require patrons to present a government-issued ID before entering the gaming floor or participating in any form of gambling. These IDs must be scrutinized closely to ensure their authenticity, which is where ID scanning technology becomes particularly useful. In earlier sections, we explored the importance of using ID scanners to verify the security features embedded within state-issued IDs, such as holograms, watermarks, and barcodes. These scanners play an equally important role in casinos, where manual inspections of IDs can sometimes lead to human error. ID scanners help verify that an ID is authentic by detecting specific features that are hard to replicate in counterfeit documents. Additionally, this technology can automatically verify the patron's age, thereby minimizing the risk of allowing underage individuals to participate in gambling activities.

Another critical area of ID verification in casinos is the implementation of anti-money laundering (AML) protocols. Casinos are considered high-risk environments for money laundering due to the large amounts of cash that flow through them daily. Therefore, both federal and state regulations require casinos to have robust systems in place for monitoring financial transactions and verifying the identity of customers who engage in large cash exchanges or transactions over a certain threshold. The Bank Secrecy Act (BSA), a key federal law governing AML regulations, mandates that casinos verify the identity of any patron making transactions of $10,000 or more and report these transactions to the Financial Crimes Enforcement Network (FinCEN). This means that ID verification is not just about checking a person's age but also ensuring that their identity is accurately documented for financial tracking purposes. If a casino fails to properly verify the identity of patrons involved in high-value transactions, it risks facing significant legal consequences, including fines and sanctions from federal authorities.

The use of ID verification systems in the gambling industry must also take into account the rise of online casinos, where the challenges of confirming a person's identity are even more complex. Unlike physical casinos where a person's ID can be scanned and visually inspected, online casinos must rely on digital verification tools to ensure that customers are of legal age and are not using fraudulent identities. The previous section on ID verification for online retail sales emphasized the importance of using secure and reliable online verification methods, a principle that applies equally in the context of online gambling. Digital ID verification systems often involve the customer uploading a scan or photograph of their ID, which is then compared against a database of valid IDs to confirm its authenticity. Some online casinos also use biometric verification, such as facial recognition, to ensure that the person submitting the ID is the same individual depicted in the document. These technologies are crucial for preventing identity fraud and ensuring that patrons are legally allowed to gamble.

However, even with advanced technology, online casinos face the risk of individuals attempting to circumvent the verification process. For example, a person might use someone else's ID to gain access to an online gambling platform or manipulate their personal details in an attempt to bypass age restrictions. As highlighted earlier in the section on limitations of ID scanning technology, no system is completely immune to fraud. Casinos must, therefore, complement their digital ID verification processes with other safeguards, such as multi-factor authentication (MFA) and continuous monitoring of user activity. This helps to detect any suspicious behavior that might indicate fraud or an attempt to bypass the ID verification process. By combining these measures with rigorous ID checks, online casinos can reduce the risk of fraudulent activity and maintain compliance with legal requirements.

Additionally, casinos must be mindful of data privacy concerns when collecting and storing personal information from IDs. The process of verifying a patron's identity often involves collecting sensitive information, such as their name, address, and date of birth, which is protected under various privacy laws. The previously mentioned California Consumer Privacy Act (CCPA), for example, grants individuals the right to know what personal information is being collected and how it is used. Casinos, especially those operating online, must ensure that they are fully compliant with such laws by obtaining consent from patrons to collect their data and ensuring that this information is stored securely. Failure to protect this data can result in significant legal penalties, including fines and lawsuits from patrons whose information has been compromised in a data breach. Therefore, implementing strong cybersecurity measures, such as encryption and regular audits, is a best practice that all casinos should follow to protect the personal information obtained through ID verification.

In the casino industry, staff training is another essential element of effective ID verification. While technology plays a significant role in verifying identities, it is ultimately the responsibility of the casino's employees to ensure that these systems are used correctly and to handle situations where additional verification may be needed. For instance, if an ID scanner flags a document as potentially fraudulent, staff must be trained to handle the situation appropriately, either by asking for a secondary form of identification or contacting management for further review. As discussed earlier in relation to other industries, employee training is crucial in reducing the likelihood of human error during the ID verification process. In a fast-paced casino environment, where patrons might present IDs from different states or countries, employees need to be well-versed in identifying the key features of various types of identification documents. This is particularly important when dealing with international guests, who may present passports or other foreign-issued documents that are less familiar to U.S. staff.

Moreover, casinos must ensure that their staff are aware of the specific legal requirements related to ID verification within their state. For instance, some states have stricter regulations on what forms of ID are acceptable for entry into a casino or participation in gambling activities. In Nevada, home to Las Vegas and one of the most heavily regulated gambling environments in the world, casinos are required to adhere to strict protocols for verifying the age and identity of patrons. Employees in these casinos must be thoroughly educated on Nevada's unique regulations, as well as federal laws such as the BSA that govern AML compliance.

ID verification in the casino and gambling industry is a multifaceted process that requires the integration of advanced technology, thorough employee training, and strict adherence to legal requirements. Whether in a physical casino or an online platform, the accurate verification of a patron's identity is essential for ensuring that the business remains compliant with age restrictions, AML regulations, and data privacy laws. As with other industries, the use of ID scanning and verification technologies can greatly enhance the accuracy and efficiency of these processes, but human oversight and continuous training remain critical to reducing the risks of fraud and non-compliance. By following these best practices, casinos can create a secure and legally compliant environment for their patrons while protecting themselves from potential legal consequences.

HOSPITALITY (HOTELS, RENTALS, ETC.)

In the hospitality industry, which includes hotels, vacation rentals, and other short-term accommodations, ID verification is a crucial aspect of business operations. Verifying a guest's identity is essential for security, legal compliance, and fraud prevention. Whether a guest is checking into a hotel or booking a vacation rental online, the process of confirming their identity ensures that the business is dealing with legitimate individuals, protects the property, and enhances the overall guest experience. In this context, ID verification practices must be both effective and efficient, while adhering to the specific legal requirements of the industry. Similar to the practices discussed in previous sections, the methods used for verifying IDs in hospitality are evolving alongside technology, and businesses must stay current to avoid compliance issues or exposure to risks.

At the heart of ID verification in the hospitality industry is the need for security. Hotels, for example, handle large numbers of guests on a daily basis, many of whom are strangers to the property and its staff. Ensuring that the individuals who check in are who they claim to be is fundamental for maintaining a secure environment. When guests present identification during check-in, whether in the form of a driver's license, passport, or other government-issued ID, it allows the hotel to confirm the legitimacy of the reservation and the identity of the person occupying the room. This is especially important for preventing unauthorized access, such as situations where individuals attempt to check in under false identities or use stolen credit cards to book rooms. In the section on retail ID verification, the importance of using reliable methods to confirm identity was emphasized, and this principle holds just as true in the hospitality industry, where the stakes for security breaches can be high.

In addition to security concerns, there are legal requirements that dictate ID verification in hospitality. Hotels, vacation rentals, and similar businesses must comply with state and federal regulations regarding guest identification. For instance, in many states, hotels are required to collect and retain certain guest information for a specified period, which often includes the details found on a government-issued ID. This information is necessary not only for tracking and billing purposes but also for law enforcement, should the need arise. In some jurisdictions, hotels are even obligated to share guest information with authorities for security or immigration purposes. For example, hotels located near international borders or in areas with higher risks of crime or terrorism may be subject to stricter ID verification requirements. These regulations are in place to protect public safety, and failure to comply can result in fines, legal action, and reputational damage to the business.

Online vacation rental platforms such as Airbnb and Vrbo present another layer of complexity in ID verification. Unlike traditional hotels, where guests physically present their ID upon check-in, vacation rentals are often booked entirely online, making it more challenging to confirm the identity of guests before they arrive. Digital ID verification tools, therefore, play a key role in this sector. These tools typically require guests to upload a scan or photo of their government-issued ID, which is then cross-referenced with databases to confirm its authenticity. Some platforms go a step further by incorporating facial recognition technology to ensure that the person booking the rental is the same as the individual depicted on the ID. As discussed earlier in the section on online ID verification for retail and alcohol sales, the rise of digital platforms has increased the need for businesses to adopt reliable, secure verification methods that can function remotely. In the context of vacation rentals, where the property owner might not meet the guest face-to-face, the importance of robust digital verification systems cannot be overstated.

In both traditional hotels and vacation rentals, fraud prevention is a significant concern. ID verification serves as a crucial line of defense against fraudulent bookings, where individuals use stolen credit cards, false identities, or fake IDs to reserve rooms or properties. This type of fraud not only leads to financial losses for the business but can also result in damage to property and safety risks for other guests. As technology continues to evolve, so do the methods that fraudsters use to circumvent verification processes. For example, high-quality fake IDs are more accessible than ever before, making it imperative for businesses in the hospitality industry to use advanced ID scanning technology that can detect even the most sophisticated forgeries. The earlier section on the limitations of ID scanners in high-risk industries like gambling highlights the need for hospitality businesses to regularly update their verification systems to keep pace with advancements in fraudulent techniques.

Another key consideration in the hospitality industry is the protection of personal data. When hotels or vacation rental platforms collect ID information, they are often handling sensitive personal data, including names, addresses, and dates of birth, which must be stored and processed in accordance with privacy laws such as the General Data Protection Regulation (GDPR) and the California Consumer Privacy Act (CCPA). As mentioned in previous sections, businesses that collect personal data must ensure that they have the proper security protocols in place to protect this information from unauthorized access or breaches. In hospitality, where guest data is often stored electronically for booking, billing, and check-in purposes, ensuring data security is critical to maintaining trust with guests. Encryption, secure databases, and restricted access are all best practices that can help prevent data breaches and protect guests' privacy.

One challenge specific to the hospitality industry is the need to balance stringent security measures with a seamless guest experience. Unlike industries such as gambling or retail, where the primary focus is on compliance and fraud prevention, the hospitality industry places a high value on customer service. Guests expect the check-in process to be smooth and efficient, and overly intrusive ID verification procedures can lead to frustration and dissatisfaction. Therefore, hotels and vacation rental platforms must strike a balance between thorough ID checks and a guest-friendly process. This can be achieved by using advanced technologies that allow for quick and accurate ID scanning or verification without causing delays. For instance, many hotels now employ self-check-in kiosks that use ID scanning technology, allowing guests to verify their identity and receive their room key without needing to wait in line at the front desk. As discussed earlier, the integration of technology into ID verification processes can streamline operations, reduce human error, and enhance customer satisfaction, which is especially important in the hospitality sector.

In some cases, hospitality businesses may encounter situations where guests present alternative forms of identification, such as military IDs or international passports. This is particularly common in hotels located near military bases or in tourist destinations that attract international visitors. Staff must be trained to recognize and verify these different forms of ID, which may not always be compatible with standard ID scanning technology. In these instances, visual inspection of the ID may be necessary, requiring staff to be knowledgeable about the features and security elements of various types of identification. As previously highlighted in sections about staff training in other industries, thorough and ongoing training for hospitality employees is critical to ensuring that they can accurately verify a wide range of ID types, even those that may not be familiar or commonly presented.

Beyond verifying a guest's identity for security and legal compliance, there are additional benefits to implementing strong ID verification practices in the hospitality industry. For example, hotels and vacation rental platforms can use verified guest information to create personalized experiences, enhance loyalty programs, and offer targeted services. Verified guest data can also help businesses prevent issues such as double bookings or unauthorized room access. By ensuring that each guest's identity is properly verified, hospitality businesses can reduce operational errors and improve the overall efficiency of their services.

ID verification in the hospitality industry is a multifaceted process that serves multiple purposes, from ensuring security and legal compliance to preventing fraud and protecting guest data. As with other industries, the best practices for ID verification in hospitality involve a combination of advanced technology, comprehensive staff training, and adherence to evolving legal requirements. Whether in a traditional hotel or an online vacation rental platform, the accurate verification of a guest's identity is critical to maintaining a safe, secure, and trustworthy business environment. As discussed in earlier sections, the importance of keeping up with the latest technological advancements and regulatory changes cannot be overstated, particularly in an industry as dynamic and guest-focused as hospitality. By following these best practices, businesses can not only protect themselves from legal and financial risks but also enhance the overall guest experience, ensuring that their operations run smoothly and efficiently.

FINANCIAL SERVICES

In the financial services industry, ID verification is a cornerstone of operations, given its crucial role in preventing fraud, complying with legal regulations, and ensuring the security of both financial institutions and their clients. Whether it is for opening bank accounts, processing loans, or facilitating large transactions, accurate identification is mandatory to protect against illicit activities such as money laundering, identity theft, and financing terrorism. As the financial industry becomes increasingly digitized, businesses within this sector must adopt best practices for ID verification that combine the effectiveness of traditional methods with the efficiency of modern technology, all while staying compliant with the ever-evolving legal landscape.

The primary reason why ID verification in the financial sector is so critical is that financial institutions, such as banks, credit unions, and investment firms, handle vast amounts of sensitive personal and financial data. Ensuring that individuals or entities conducting transactions or opening accounts are exactly who they claim to be is essential to maintaining the integrity of the system. As discussed in earlier sections on retail and hospitality, where identity verification plays a key role in safeguarding transactions and preventing fraud, the financial services industry demands an even higher level of scrutiny. This heightened level of attention stems from the direct connection between financial activities and the potential for serious criminal activities, including money laundering and fraud. Therefore, regulatory bodies such as the U.S. Department of the Treasury's Financial Crimes Enforcement Network (FinCEN) and the Office of Foreign Assets Control (OFAC) have stringent requirements in place that compel financial institutions to implement thorough ID verification processes.

The Bank Secrecy Act (BSA) and the USA PATRIOT Act are two foundational regulations that mandate how financial institutions should handle ID verification. Both acts require institutions to identify and verify the identities of their clients, especially in transactions that involve significant sums of money or other high-risk factors. One of the key provisions of the USA PATRIOT Act is the Customer Identification Program (CIP), which requires all financial institutions to have a system in place that collects information such as the name, address, date of birth, and identification number (such as a Social Security number) of any individual opening an account. Verifying these details often involves cross-referencing the information with government-issued IDs, such as a driver's license or passport, to ensure that the person is legitimate and has not been flagged for suspicious activity. As previously discussed in relation to ID verification in other high-risk industries like casinos, the stakes are high in financial services, and failure to verify an individual's identity can result in severe penalties for the institution, including fines and loss of reputation.

One of the most effective tools for ID verification in financial services is the use of technology, especially in an era where digital transactions are on the rise. Many financial institutions now rely on sophisticated software systems that automatically verify a client's identity by checking the security features of government-issued IDs, such as holograms, barcodes, and other embedded features. These systems can instantly cross-reference an ID with a national or international database to ensure that it has not been reported as lost, stolen, or otherwise invalid. This process, which echoes the ID scanning technology used in retail and hospitality, allows for both speed and accuracy, which is essential in today's fast-paced financial environment. Moreover, online and mobile banking services, which have grown in popularity, require financial institutions to adopt even more advanced digital ID verification solutions, including biometric verification, such as fingerprint or facial recognition, to ensure that users accessing sensitive financial data are authorized to do so.

As with any digital solution, there are risks and limitations, particularly when it comes to the increasing sophistication of fraudulent schemes. Financial criminals have become adept at creating high-quality counterfeit IDs or using synthetic identities, which combine real and fake information to create a new, fraudulent identity. This is where the financial services industry must be vigilant in employing multi-layered verification systems that go beyond simply scanning an ID. These systems may include cross-checking ID details with other sources of information, such as credit reports, utility bills, or financial history, to verify a person's identity more comprehensively. Similar to the processes used in the casino industry, where large sums of money are exchanged, financial institutions must ensure that their ID verification processes are not only thorough but also continually updated to keep up with the latest fraud tactics.

Another best practice in ID verification for financial services involves training employees to recognize the warning signs of potential fraud. While technology plays a critical role in verifying IDs, the human element is equally important in this sector, especially when dealing with high-risk transactions or clients with complex financial histories. Employees should be trained to look for inconsistencies in identification documents, such as mismatched addresses or altered photos, as well as behaviors that might indicate suspicious activity, such as reluctance to provide necessary information or attempts to bypass verification procedures. As discussed in earlier sections related to staff training in hospitality and other industries, human oversight remains a key component of the ID verification process. In financial services, this oversight is crucial not only for identifying fraudulent activities but also for ensuring compliance with regulatory requirements.

In addition to preventing fraud, ID verification in financial services is necessary for maintaining compliance with anti-money laundering (AML) regulations. Financial institutions are required to monitor large or suspicious transactions and report them to FinCEN through a process known as Suspicious Activity Reporting (SAR). Part of this process involves verifying the identities of individuals or entities making large deposits, withdrawals, or transfers. If a client attempts to conduct a transaction that exceeds the threshold set by AML regulations, typically $10,000 or more, the financial institution must not only verify their identity but also document the transaction and any relevant details for reporting purposes. Failure to follow these AML guidelines can result in hefty fines and, in extreme cases, criminal charges against the financial institution for facilitating money laundering, even unintentionally. As with the legal obligations faced by other industries, such as gambling, financial institutions must be meticulous in how they verify client identities and document transactions to avoid regulatory breaches.

Online financial services and the rise of fintech (financial technology) companies present additional challenges in ID verification. Unlike traditional banks, which often rely on in-person interactions for identity verification, fintech platforms operate predominantly online, where verifying a user's identity can be more difficult. To combat this, fintech companies must leverage digital ID verification solutions that are as secure as they are user-friendly. Biometric verification, digital signatures, and artificial intelligence (AI) are all tools that fintech companies use to confirm a client's identity in real-time while ensuring that the verification process does not hinder the user experience. For instance, some platforms use AI-driven algorithms to analyze a user's photo ID and compare it with a live selfie to ensure that the person signing up is the same as the one depicted on the ID. These technologies are vital in helping fintech companies stay compliant with regulatory requirements while offering the convenience of online financial services.

However, the use of technology in ID verification must always be balanced with a strong commitment to protecting personal data. As financial institutions and fintech companies collect sensitive information, such as Social Security numbers, addresses, and financial records, they must adhere to data privacy laws like the General Data Protection Regulation (GDPR) and the California Consumer Privacy Act (CCPA). These laws require businesses to implement strict data protection measures, obtain explicit consent from clients before collecting personal data, and ensure that this data is securely stored and not misused. As previously discussed in the context of other industries that handle personal information, such as hospitality, maintaining compliance with privacy laws is critical to preserving client trust and avoiding legal penalties. Financial institutions, in particular, must take extra precautions to protect the vast amounts of sensitive data they handle during the ID verification process.

Best practices for ID verification in the financial services industry involve a combination of technological solutions, employee training, and strict adherence to legal and regulatory requirements. Whether it is preventing fraud, complying with AML regulations, or protecting personal data, financial institutions must ensure that their ID verification processes are robust, up-to-date, and capable of adapting to new challenges as the financial landscape continues to evolve. By employing these best practices, financial institutions can protect themselves and their clients from the risks of identity theft, fraud, and non-compliance, while fostering trust and security in their services. As highlighted in earlier sections, the integration of advanced technology with human oversight is essential for creating a comprehensive approach to ID verification, particularly in industries like financial services where accuracy and security are paramount.

AIRPORTS AND TRAVEL

In the context of airports and travel, ID verification is an essential process that ensures the security of passengers, personnel, and assets. The procedures involved in verifying identification documents at airports must be both meticulous and efficient, as they play a critical role in safeguarding air travel and national security. Airports and travel industries follow stringent guidelines for ID verification to prevent unauthorized access, identify potential threats, and confirm the authenticity of passengers, all while balancing the need for speed and convenience. These procedures must align with state and federal regulations and integrate with the technological systems already in place to achieve a streamlined and effective process.

One of the most crucial aspects of ID verification in airports is compliance with the Transportation Security Administration (TSA) guidelines. The TSA outlines specific requirements for acceptable forms of identification, such as passports, state-issued driver's licenses, or other federally recognized ID cards. Passengers are required to present these documents at various checkpoints, including check-in counters, security screening points, and boarding gates. The goal is to establish the identity of each passenger to ensure that they are not on a watchlist or prohibited from flying. In airports, the margin for error is minimal, so it is critical that staff members are trained to recognize and authenticate a wide range of ID formats from across the country and, in some cases, internationally.

Technological advancements play a central role in modern ID verification processes within the travel industry. Airports have integrated systems such as biometric scanners, facial recognition technology, and automated ID readers that link with government databases. These technologies enhance accuracy by quickly cross-referencing passenger information against national and international records. For example, facial recognition systems match the passenger's face to the photo on their ID, while the database checks provide additional verification of the document's validity and the traveler's status. This combination of technology helps to reduce the reliance on human assessment alone, minimizing errors and expediting the verification process. The integration of these technologies aligns with best practices outlined in a previous section discussing the importance of using advanced technological tools for ID validation to achieve both efficiency and high accuracy.

At security checkpoints, TSA officers and airport personnel are trained to identify tampered or fraudulent documents. This training includes detailed instruction on examining security features embedded in state and federal IDs, such as holograms, UV-sensitive elements, microprinting, and watermarks. The staff's ability to discern the legitimacy of these security features is critical in detecting forgeries and preventing unauthorized access. Training programs must be updated regularly to keep up with evolving forgery techniques and advancements in ID technology. Previous sections emphasize the importance of continuous training in ID verification to ensure that personnel are well-equipped to recognize any irregularities quickly and accurately.

In addition to document inspection, airports also prioritize the consistency of ID verification procedures across different points of contact. Passengers encounter multiple verification points before boarding, including airline check-in desks, TSA security checks, and boarding gates. Consistent verification processes are essential to maintaining a high level of security throughout the passenger's journey. A lapse at any point could compromise the entire system. Therefore, collaboration between airline staff and TSA agents is critical to ensuring that the standards and practices of ID verification are uniform and effective.

Another key best practice in the travel industry is ensuring that ID verification processes remain adaptable to different scenarios, including accommodating international travelers. For example, airports regularly handle passengers with non-U.S. passports or travel documents. As these documents may vary in format and security features, airport personnel must be trained to recognize different types of international identification, including those issued by foreign governments. In addition to basic document inspection skills, officers should have access to up-to-date guides or databases that detail the specifications of international IDs. This approach is consistent with strategies discussed in a previous section that recommended maintaining up-to-date resources for personnel, ensuring they can verify documents issued by different states and jurisdictions with confidence and accuracy.

Another important aspect of ID verification in airports is the need for measures that can manage high passenger volumes efficiently. During peak travel times, such as holidays or major events, airports may see a surge in passenger numbers, increasing the demand for efficient ID checks. To manage this, airports often implement automated solutions like e-gates and biometric kiosks. These systems not only expedite the verification process but also enhance accuracy by reducing the potential for human error. For example, automated ID readers scan barcodes or chip-enabled IDs and verify passenger information against databases within seconds, allowing for quicker processing and reducing wait times. E-gates equipped with facial recognition technology provide a seamless experience where passengers scan their ID, and the system automatically matches the information to the person's face, minimizing the need for manual intervention.

Additionally, airports employ layered security measures to validate the identity of employees and other personnel who have access to restricted areas. Employee IDs are also subjected to verification processes similar to those for passengers but may involve additional security checks, such as background screenings and biometric authentication. Access to secure zones is often regulated through advanced security systems, including badge readers and biometric checkpoints, ensuring that only authorized personnel can enter. Training for personnel to recognize fellow staff members' ID cards and security badges is another crucial component of ensuring a secure environment. This is consistent with sections in previous sections that highlighted the importance of maintaining secure environments through rigorous verification and training.

Data privacy is another critical component in the ID verification process at airports. Since sensitive personal information is processed during ID checks, airports must comply with data protection regulations to prevent unauthorized access or misuse of information. For instance, airports need to follow the guidelines set forth by the Department of Homeland Security (DHS) and the TSA regarding data storage, access, and management. This includes ensuring that databases are encrypted, access to sensitive information is restricted to authorized personnel only, and records are kept secure. Furthermore, airports must have protocols in place for disposing of personal data that is no longer needed, ensuring compliance with privacy laws. Staff members are trained on these protocols to maintain the integrity and confidentiality of passenger information.

In light of the Real ID Act, which mandates that all states issue compliant driver's licenses and ID cards by specific deadlines, airports must ensure that their systems are up-to-date to recognize these IDs. Passengers who present non-compliant IDs may face additional screening procedures or may be denied access to secure areas. It is essential for airport personnel to be aware of which states are compliant and the features that distinguish Real ID-compliant documents from non-compliant ones. This knowledge allows staff to provide clear guidance to passengers and ensure compliance with federal regulations. The importance of keeping verification systems up-to-date with current laws and regulations is a theme echoed in previous sections, where the necessity of staying aligned with legal requirements was discussed in depth.

Airports also coordinate closely with law enforcement agencies and international security organizations to improve ID verification processes. Collaboration with these entities allows airports to access databases and share information on potential threats or individuals of concern. When a passenger's ID is flagged during verification, airport personnel work with law enforcement to resolve the situation swiftly and securely, ensuring that the threat is contained while minimizing disruption to other passengers. This coordinated approach ensures that airport security remains robust and responsive to potential risks.

Effective communication with passengers is another vital component in ensuring successful ID verification in the travel industry. Clear signage and instructions throughout the airport help passengers understand what is expected of them at each checkpoint. Announcements and staff guidance are crucial in directing passengers to have their documents ready and ensuring a smooth flow through security checks. Moreover, providing information on acceptable forms of identification and TSA requirements in advance through airline websites, apps, and pre-travel communications helps passengers prepare before arriving at the airport, thereby minimizing delays and confusion.

By implementing these best practices, the travel industry ensures a balance between security and efficiency, reducing the risk of unauthorized access while accommodating the high volume of passengers that pass through airports daily. Continuous improvement, collaboration, and technological integration remain central to the success of ID verification processes in the airport and travel sector.

PART 4

Legal and Ethical Considerations

CHAPTER 10

FEDERAL AND STATE LAWS GOVERNING ID CHECKS

OVERVIEW OF FEDERAL ID LAWS

Federal laws play a central role in establishing the standards and regulations surrounding ID checks in the United States. These laws are designed to ensure that identification processes across different states and industries are consistent, secure, and reliable. They establish the framework for both public and private entities to follow when verifying the identities of individuals, aiming to prevent fraud, protect privacy, and enhance national security. Understanding these laws is crucial for organizations that must comply with them, as non-compliance can lead to severe legal consequences, penalties, or compromised security. By adhering to federal guidelines, entities not only fulfill their legal obligations but also contribute to a broader system of safety and trust.

One of the most influential pieces of legislation governing ID checks in the United States is the Real ID Act of 2005. Passed in response to the 9/11 Commission's recommendation for increased identity security, the Real ID Act sets stringent requirements for state-issued driver's licenses and identification cards to be recognized as valid federal IDs. The act establishes minimum security standards for these documents, such as the inclusion of anti-counterfeiting features, digital photographs, and specific demographic information. States are required to verify the identity and legal status of individuals before issuing a Real ID-compliant card. As previously discussed in the section on best practices for ID verification in the travel industry, the Real ID Act directly impacts airports, as only Real ID-compliant IDs or other federally accepted documents (such as passports) are valid for domestic air travel. This mandate highlights the federal government's commitment to tightening security measures and minimizing the use of fraudulent or invalid identification.

In addition to the Real ID Act, the Immigration Reform and Control Act (IRCA) of 1986 is another key federal law that influences ID checks, particularly within the employment sector. This law requires employers to verify the identity and legal work authorization of every new employee, regardless of citizenship status. Employers must complete Form I-9, which serves as a record that they have reviewed and verified an employee's documents proving identity and employment eligibility. The IRCA's requirements are reinforced by the Department of Homeland Security (DHS) through audits and compliance checks, making it essential for businesses to understand and implement effective ID verification practices. As referenced in earlier sections regarding the importance of accurate verification, the consequences of failing to comply with the IRCA can include fines, sanctions, and, in severe cases, criminal charges. This underscores the critical need for employers to be well-versed in federal requirements and maintain rigorous ID checking protocols.

The USA PATRIOT Act, enacted in 2001, is another significant piece of legislation impacting ID verification processes. This law expanded the government's ability to monitor and prevent activities linked to terrorism and other serious threats by enhancing identification and reporting requirements for financial institutions and other regulated entities. Under the PATRIOT Act, banks and other financial institutions are required to implement Customer Identification Programs (CIP) as part of their anti-money laundering (AML) compliance measures. These programs mandate that financial entities verify the identity of individuals conducting transactions and maintain records of their identification documents. For instance, when a new customer opens an account, the institution must verify their name, date of birth, and social security number or other federally issued identification. This legal framework ensures that financial institutions are vigilant in preventing identity theft, money laundering, and the financing of terrorism. This aligns with the best practices discussed in earlier sections that highlight the use of multi-layered approaches to identity verification, emphasizing the need for combining document inspection with database checks and other authentication methods.

The Driver's Privacy Protection Act (DPPA) of 1994 is another federal law that significantly influences the handling of state-issued IDs, particularly driver's licenses. The DPPA regulates how motor vehicle departments and other organizations can collect, store, and share the personal information associated with state-issued driver's licenses and identification cards. It restricts access to this data to protect individuals' privacy while still allowing for certain authorized uses, such as by law enforcement agencies or entities verifying an individual's identity for approved purposes. The DPPA is especially important for businesses that rely on verifying driver's licenses as part of their customer identification processes, such as rental agencies, financial institutions, and law firms. The law mandates that these entities must adhere to privacy standards when accessing and using this information, ensuring that personal data is not misused or shared unlawfully. In the context of the broader section on ID verification protocols, the DPPA highlights the balance between security and privacy, ensuring that entities respect individuals' personal information while still maintaining rigorous verification processes.

The Federal Trade Commission (FTC) also plays a role in governing ID checks through the implementation of the Red Flags Rule, part of the Fair and Accurate Credit Transactions Act (FACTA) of 2003. The Red Flags Rule requires financial institutions and creditors to develop, implement, and administer an Identity Theft Prevention Program designed to detect, prevent, and mitigate identity theft. This involves establishing policies to identify warning signs—known as "red flags"—that may indicate potential identity theft, such as discrepancies in identification documents or suspicious account activities. The Red Flags Rule emphasizes the importance of ongoing monitoring and the need for businesses to have procedures in place to respond swiftly when a red flag is detected. This law underscores the federal government's focus on preemptive measures in identity verification, aiming to protect both consumers and organizations from the consequences of identity theft. The relevance of these proactive measures ties back to earlier sections on the necessity for continuous vigilance and regular updates to ID verification practices, especially as threats and fraudulent tactics evolve.

The Health Insurance Portability and Accountability Act (HIPAA) also intersects with ID checks, particularly in healthcare settings where identity verification is crucial to protect patient information and ensure compliance with privacy standards. HIPAA mandates that healthcare providers verify the identity of patients before accessing or disclosing sensitive health information. This means that healthcare facilities must use stringent ID verification processes, such as checking state-issued IDs or other valid documents, to confirm that patients are who they claim to be. HIPAA also requires that healthcare entities maintain secure records of identification checks and that they only share patient information with authorized parties. This law reinforces the need for healthcare facilities to balance accessibility with privacy, ensuring that proper identification methods are followed without compromising the security of patient data.

In the context of transportation and national security, the federal government has enacted laws like the Aviation and Transportation Security Act (ATSA) of 2001, which established the Transportation

Security Administration (TSA). The TSA is responsible for implementing and enforcing ID verification standards at airports across the country, ensuring that only properly identified and vetted individuals gain access to secure areas and board flights. This act, which aligns closely with the Real ID Act, mandates that travelers present valid identification documents that meet federal security standards. The TSA's enforcement of these laws is critical to maintaining airport security and preventing unauthorized access or threats. The previous section on the integration of technological systems in airports illustrates how federal laws like the ATSA shape ID verification procedures by requiring the use of advanced methods such as biometrics, automated readers, and real-time database checks.

Federal ID laws extend beyond the realms of travel, finance, and healthcare to cover industries such as alcohol and tobacco sales. The Alcohol and Tobacco Tax and Trade Bureau (TTB), operating under the Department of the Treasury, enforces laws that require sellers of alcohol and tobacco products to verify the age and identity of customers before completing a sale. The aim is to prevent underage sales and ensure compliance with state and federal age restrictions. Sellers must use valid, government-issued identification as proof of age, and failure to do so can result in fines, penalties, or the revocation of licenses. This highlights the importance of ID verification processes in regulated industries and reinforces the broader federal mandate to protect public safety through rigorous and consistent identity checks.

Federal laws governing ID checks are comprehensive and detailed, covering various industries and scenarios where identity verification is critical. These laws ensure that entities across the United States maintain consistent, high standards in verifying individuals' identities, reducing the risk of fraud, identity theft, and threats to public safety. By adhering to these federal requirements, organizations not only protect themselves from legal consequences but also contribute to a national system of security and trust that benefits both individuals and society as a whole.

IMPORTANT STATE-LEVEL ID VERIFICATION REGULATIONS

State-level ID verification regulations across the United States are diverse and often reflect the individual needs, priorities, and laws specific to each state. These regulations establish standards for issuing, verifying, and accepting various forms of identification, including driver's licenses, state ID cards, and other officially recognized documents. While federal laws such as the Real ID Act set a baseline for compliance, each state has its own set of rules and procedures that can affect how identification documents are managed and verified. Understanding these nuances is essential for any organization involved in ID verification, as it ensures compliance with state regulations and minimizes the risk of legal repercussions or security breaches.

In Alabama, the state's Department of Public Safety sets requirements for driver's licenses and ID cards, incorporating features like holograms, barcodes, and digital signatures to prevent tampering and forgery. Alabama's regulations emphasize strict verification processes, including proof of residency and legal presence, ensuring that only eligible individuals receive state-issued IDs. Similarly, Alaska has specific laws that require additional scrutiny for residents in rural areas, where verifying physical addresses can be more challenging. Alaska's regulations also accommodate the state's unique geographic and cultural landscape by providing alternative means of verification for individuals living in remote regions.

Arizona's ID laws reflect its proximity to an international border, requiring enhanced verification procedures for driver's licenses and state IDs. Arizona offers an "Enhanced Driver's License" (EDL) option, which includes RFID technology and is compliant with federal border-crossing requirements, demonstrating how state laws can integrate with federal mandates for increased security. Meanwhile, Arkansas enforces stringent requirements for age verification, particularly in the context of alcohol and tobacco sales, with regulations mandating that retailers use state-approved ID verification technologies. These measures align with sections in earlier sections about the importance of technology in maintaining the accuracy and reliability of ID checks.

California's ID verification regulations are among the most comprehensive in the nation, requiring biometric data such as thumbprints for certain types of licenses and IDs. California's Department of Motor Vehicles (DMV) also has specific protocols for verifying the identity of undocumented immigrants, offering a "California AB 60" license that allows residents without legal status to obtain a driver's license, provided they meet certain criteria and pass extensive verification procedures. In contrast, Colorado emphasizes the security features of its state IDs, including ultraviolet images and microtext that can be detected only through specialized equipment, enhancing its ability to combat counterfeiting and fraud.

Connecticut's laws include stringent protocols for verifying Social Security numbers and proof of legal residency before issuing any form of identification. The state also participates actively in the federal Systematic Alien Verification for Entitlements (SAVE) program, which helps verify the legal status of non-citizens applying for state-issued IDs. Delaware's DMV incorporates facial recognition technology as part of its ID issuance process, using biometric data to cross-check new applicants with existing records to prevent identity theft and fraud, aligning with earlier sections on the role of technology in enhancing security.

Florida has specific regulations regarding the issuance of driver's licenses to seasonal residents and retirees, given its large population of non-permanent residents. Florida's laws ensure that these individuals must provide proof of residence and demonstrate their eligibility to receive a state ID. This is particularly important in states like Florida, where the demographic variations require tailored verification procedures. Georgia, meanwhile, focuses on the real-time updating of its DMV database, which allows for immediate cross-checking of new applicants against state and national criminal records, enhancing security and compliance measures.

Hawaii's ID regulations are tailored to its unique geography, including provisions for individuals living on different islands. The state uses a centralized system for processing ID applications, which helps maintain consistency and security standards despite the physical separation of its population. Idaho's regulations include the use of advanced holographic technology in its state IDs, providing multiple layers of security that help prevent forgery and duplication.

Illinois's ID verification laws emphasize the need for age verification in the purchase of age-restricted items. Retailers in Illinois must use state-approved electronic ID verification systems, particularly in alcohol, tobacco, and cannabis sales, to reduce the likelihood of minors accessing restricted products. Indiana incorporates specific requirements for military personnel and veterans, allowing them to receive specialized ID cards that grant access to military facilities while also ensuring that their information is kept secure.

Iowa's regulations involve strict background checks for individuals applying for commercial driver's licenses, with an emphasis on verifying legal status and criminal records. Kansas uses similar measures but also incorporates verification processes specific to agricultural workers, reflecting the state's economic and demographic makeup. Kentucky's DMV incorporates fingerprinting for certain types of IDs, offering an additional layer of biometric security.

Louisiana's state regulations allow the use of digital driver's licenses, which are accessible through a mobile application. This modern approach not only provides convenience for residents but also incorporates security measures like QR codes and real-time verification. Maine's ID verification laws include unique protocols for verifying residency, especially in rural and less populated areas, ensuring that residents can provide adequate proof despite geographical challenges.

Maryland's laws emphasize identity protection, including the use of encryption and secure digital storage for ID-related data. Massachusetts requires proof of citizenship or lawful presence for all state ID applicants and participates in the Real ID program to ensure its documents meet federal security standards. Michigan's regulations focus on ensuring that its state-issued IDs include enhanced security features such as laser-engraved elements, which are difficult to replicate. Minnesota has similar measures, but it also offers an EDL option to facilitate cross-border travel to Canada.

Mississippi has regulations that require comprehensive background checks for applicants applying for commercial licenses or licenses with specific endorsements. Missouri's ID verification system is linked directly to state law enforcement databases, allowing for immediate cross-referencing and identity confirmation during the issuance process. Montana uses secure digital imaging to maintain ID integrity, preventing unauthorized alterations.

Nebraska has strict residency requirements that applicants must meet to obtain state-issued IDs, including proof of continuous residence for a specified period. Nevada's state laws accommodate its transient population, requiring additional verification steps for individuals who do not have a permanent address, which ensures compliance without compromising security. New Hampshire's DMV incorporates a centralized system for real-time ID verification, connecting with other states to cross-check applicant information.

New Jersey's regulations include the implementation of facial recognition technology, providing an additional security measure to prevent identity theft and fraud. New Mexico's ID laws accommodate the state's diverse population, including provisions for undocumented residents similar to those in California. New York has comprehensive regulations, requiring all ID applicants to provide multiple forms of verification, including proof of residency, Social Security information, and legal status. The state also issues EDLs for international travel convenience.

North Carolina's ID verification regulations focus on age-restricted sales, with state-mandated electronic ID verification systems for alcohol, tobacco, and gaming establishments. North Dakota's laws include specific requirements for rural residents, providing alternative verification methods for individuals without standard forms of address documentation. Ohio's ID regulations emphasize the integration of biometric data, such as thumbprints, to strengthen the security of state IDs.

Oklahoma incorporates advanced holographic technology into its state IDs, ensuring that each document has multiple security features to detect and prevent fraud. Oregon's laws emphasize environmental considerations, using eco-friendly materials in state ID cards while maintaining high-security standards. Pennsylvania's regulations include provisions for verifying the identity of veterans, offering specialized military IDs while ensuring compliance with state and federal security guidelines.

Rhode Island's DMV uses a digital system for verifying residency and legal status, integrating this information into a state-wide database that allows for cross-referencing and secure storage. South Carolina's regulations emphasize the use of ultraviolet technology in state-issued IDs, adding a layer of security that helps prevent counterfeiting. South Dakota's ID laws are tailored to accommodate its large rural population, with provisions for verifying identity in remote areas.

Tennessee's regulations require all driver's licenses and state IDs to include multiple security features, including microprinting and secure digital imaging, to ensure authenticity. Texas's ID laws reflect the state's diverse demographic, offering different types of identification cards, including those for undocumented residents, while maintaining rigorous verification standards. Utah's ID regulations incorporate the use of advanced digital technology for ID issuance, allowing real-time verification of applicant information.

Vermont's regulations require proof of residency and lawful presence, and its state IDs include encrypted barcodes for added security. Virginia's

ID laws are tailored to accommodate federal employees and military personnel, ensuring they have access to specialized ID cards that also meet state verification standards. Washington's DMV issues EDLs that meet federal requirements for border crossing, integrating RFID technology for secure identification.

West Virginia's ID regulations include strict protocols for verifying Social Security numbers and proof of residence, ensuring compliance with both state and federal guidelines. Wisconsin's state ID laws focus on secure storage and encryption of applicant information, while Wyoming's regulations incorporate advanced imaging technology for secure ID production, ensuring the integrity of state-issued documents.

Each state's unique ID verification regulations reflect the local priorities, demographics, and legal landscapes within the broader framework set by federal laws. This diversity emphasizes the importance of understanding state-specific requirements for businesses and organizations involved in ID verification, ensuring compliance while maintaining high levels of security and reliability. By aligning state practices with federal guidelines and continuously updating these regulations to respond to emerging threats and technologies, states contribute to the collective effort of maintaining a secure and effective ID verification system nationwide.

CHAPTER 11

PRIVACY AND DATA PROTECTION

HANDLING PERSONAL INFORMATION SAFELY

Handling personal information safely is a critical responsibility for any entity involved in ID verification, whether it be businesses, government agencies, or other organizations. The protection of personal data is not only a legal obligation under various state and federal laws but also an ethical imperative to maintain trust and security in the ID verification process. Given the increasing threats of data breaches, identity theft, and unauthorized access to sensitive information, entities must adopt robust procedures and technologies to safeguard personal information effectively. A comprehensive approach to managing personal data requires understanding the principles of privacy, employing appropriate security measures, and adhering to legal regulations that govern the storage, handling, and disposal of sensitive information.

The first step in safely handling personal information is understanding the nature of the data being collected and verified. Personal information includes any data that can be used to identify an individual, such as full name, date of birth, address, Social Security number, driver's license number, and biometric data like fingerprints or facial recognition data. The collection of this information often happens during the ID verification process, as seen in various industries including travel, finance, healthcare, and retail. In earlier sections about the application of biometric technology in ID verification, it was highlighted how important it is for organizations to use this data securely, as it represents a highly sensitive and personally identifiable form of information. Organizations must ensure that they are only collecting the minimum necessary data to perform identity verification tasks, thereby reducing the risk of exposing unnecessary information.

Once personal information is collected, it is essential to store it securely. Secure storage involves implementing both physical and digital measures to prevent unauthorized access. Digital information should be stored in encrypted databases that are protected by advanced security protocols, including firewalls, secure access controls, and regular monitoring for vulnerabilities. Encryption is a fundamental component, as it transforms sensitive data into unreadable code that can only be accessed or decrypted by authorized personnel with the proper keys. Encryption protects data at rest and in transit, ensuring that even if the information is intercepted or accessed by unauthorized individuals, it remains secure. In addition to encryption, organizations should use multi-factor authentication (MFA) systems for access to sensitive information, ensuring that only authorized employees can retrieve or modify personal data.

Physical security measures are also crucial in handling personal information safely. Offices and data centers where personal information is stored should have controlled access, such as keycard systems, security personnel, and surveillance cameras. These measures prevent unauthorized individuals from accessing physical files or hardware that contain sensitive data. Furthermore, documents and devices that store personal information should be kept in secure locations, such as locked cabinets or safes, and only accessible to authorized staff. Organizations must also establish clear policies and protocols for the disposal of physical records containing personal information. For instance, shredding documents or securely deleting electronic records ensures that no residual data is left accessible after the information is no longer needed.

Organizations must also be proactive in maintaining data security through regular audits, system updates, and employee training. Regular audits help identify vulnerabilities in the storage and handling of personal information, allowing entities to address potential risks before they are exploited. These audits should include both physical and digital security assessments, ensuring that all measures are functioning as intended. Regular software and system updates are equally important, as they provide patches for known vulnerabilities and enhance the overall security of data storage systems. Training employees on the importance of data privacy and security is another critical element of managing personal information safely. Employees should be familiar with the protocols for handling sensitive data, the legal requirements surrounding privacy, and the best practices for preventing breaches, such as recognizing phishing attempts or other social engineering tactics that could compromise security.

Another vital aspect of handling personal information safely is compliance with federal and state regulations that govern data privacy and protection. Federal laws such as the Health Insurance Portability and Accountability Act (HIPAA), the Fair Credit Reporting Act (FCRA), and the Gramm-Leach-Bliley Act (GLBA) establish guidelines for organizations handling personal information in healthcare, financial, and other industries. HIPAA, for example, requires healthcare providers to implement specific security measures when handling and storing patient information, ensuring that only authorized personnel have access and that data is encrypted during storage and transmission. This aligns with earlier sections on healthcare ID verification and the role of HIPAA in ensuring that patient data remains secure throughout the verification process. Similarly, the GLBA mandates that financial institutions develop and maintain policies for safeguarding customer information, demonstrating the importance of compliance in protecting personal information.

State-level regulations also play a critical role in shaping how organizations manage personal data. For example, California's Consumer Privacy Act (CCPA) gives residents the right to know what personal information businesses collect about them and mandates that businesses implement security measures to protect that data. The CCPA also provides consumers with the right to request deletion of their data and the ability to opt out of the sale of their information. This law underscores the importance of transparency and accountability, ensuring that consumers have control over their personal information and that businesses are held responsible for protecting it. The New York SHIELD Act is another state-level regulation that requires businesses to implement reasonable safeguards for personal information, including measures for detecting and responding to data breaches. By understanding and complying with these laws, organizations can better protect personal information and avoid legal penalties.

Another critical area of focus for handling personal information safely is the development of a comprehensive data breach response plan. Despite the best efforts to secure data, breaches can still occur, and organizations must be prepared to respond quickly and effectively. A well-defined response plan includes identifying the breach source, containing the breach, assessing the impact, notifying affected individuals, and cooperating with regulatory authorities. The plan should outline the specific roles and responsibilities of team members and establish clear communication protocols to ensure a swift and coordinated response. Prompt notification of affected individuals is often legally required and is essential to maintain trust and mitigate harm. Organizations must also analyze the breach to understand how it occurred and implement corrective measures to prevent similar incidents in the future.

Given the importance of technology in the ID verification process, organizations must also be vigilant in securing the systems and software they use for managing and verifying personal information. Technologies such as facial recognition, biometric scanning, and electronic ID databases are increasingly employed to enhance the efficiency and accuracy of ID verification. As previously discussed, these technologies can significantly improve the effectiveness of verifying identities; however, they also introduce additional risks if not properly secured. It is critical for organizations to use secure, regularly updated systems that meet the highest industry standards for data protection. Regular testing and monitoring of these systems can help identify vulnerabilities and ensure that any potential threats are promptly addressed.

Privacy policies are another crucial component of handling personal information safely. Organizations must develop clear and transparent privacy policies that outline what data is collected, how it is used, who has access, and how it is protected. These policies should be communicated to customers and employees alike, ensuring that all parties understand their rights and responsibilities when it comes to managing personal data. Clear communication builds trust with consumers and provides them with confidence that their personal information is being handled responsibly. Privacy policies also serve as an internal guideline for employees, helping them understand the importance of following best practices and maintaining compliance with legal requirements.

It is essential for organizations to establish a culture of privacy and security that permeates all levels of their operations. This involves integrating privacy considerations into every aspect of the business, from the initial design of ID verification systems to the day-to-day handling of personal information by employees. Privacy by design is a proactive approach that emphasizes the incorporation of privacy features into products, services, and operational practices from the outset, rather than as an afterthought. This approach ensures that privacy and security measures are embedded into the organizational infrastructure, reducing the risk of breaches and improving the overall handling of personal information.

Handling personal information safely is a multifaceted responsibility that requires organizations to be vigilant, proactive, and compliant with legal regulations. By employing secure storage and encryption methods, implementing physical and digital security measures, conducting regular audits, training employees, and adhering to federal and state laws, entities can protect personal information and mitigate risks. Additionally, developing data breach response plans, securing technology, and establishing clear privacy policies all contribute to a comprehensive strategy for managing personal information responsibly. Organizations that prioritize these measures not only fulfill their legal obligations but also demonstrate a commitment to the trust and security of the individuals they serve, reinforcing the integrity of the ID verification process.

PROTECTING AGAINST IDENTITY THEFT

Identity theft is a pervasive and evolving threat that poses significant risks to individuals and organizations alike. It occurs when someone unlawfully acquires and uses another person's personal information, often for financial gain, fraud, or other malicious purposes. This crime can lead to severe consequences for victims, including financial loss, damaged credit, and emotional distress. For businesses and organizations involved in ID verification, understanding the various forms of identity theft and implementing protective measures is essential to safeguard the identities of those they serve. In-depth knowledge of the methods criminals use, the technologies available to detect fraudulent activity, and the best practices for preventing identity theft ensures a secure environment for both organizations and individuals.

One of the most common forms of identity theft is financial fraud, where criminals use stolen information to access bank accounts, open credit cards, or secure loans under a false identity. This can happen when sensitive data such as Social Security numbers, credit card details, or banking information is compromised. Criminals may obtain this information through various means, including data breaches, phishing scams, and skimming devices installed on ATMs or point-of-sale systems. A comprehensive approach to identity verification, as discussed in earlier sections about the implementation of technology and biometric systems, is crucial in detecting and preventing such fraudulent activities. By integrating secure technology and biometric authentication methods, organizations can make it significantly harder for identity thieves to gain unauthorized access using stolen information.

Another type of identity theft involves the misuse of personal identification to gain medical services or benefits fraudulently. Medical identity theft can result in altered medical records, leading to incorrect medical treatments for the actual patient and substantial financial liabilities. It highlights the importance of stringent ID verification processes within the healthcare sector. For healthcare providers, complying with regulations like the Health Insurance Portability and Accountability Act (HIPAA), which mandates the protection of patient information, is not only a legal requirement but also a vital step in preventing identity theft. As explored previously in the context of state and federal laws governing ID checks, ensuring compliance with these regulations provides an essential layer of protection against identity theft in medical contexts.

Another concern is tax identity theft, where criminals use stolen Social Security numbers and other personal information to file fraudulent tax returns and claim refunds in someone else's name. This form of theft has become increasingly common as more people file their taxes electronically. To combat this, the IRS has implemented additional security measures such as personal identification numbers (PINs) for taxpayers, but businesses and individuals must also be vigilant in protecting their data. For organizations responsible for verifying identities in contexts where Social Security numbers are collected, safeguarding this information through encryption and other digital security measures is critical. As previously discussed in relation to digital storage solutions and encryption, these practices are fundamental to maintaining the integrity and confidentiality of personal data.

Synthetic identity theft is a more sophisticated form of crime that has grown in prominence. In this scenario, criminals combine real and fictitious information to create a new identity. They might use a legitimate Social Security number, often that of a minor or an individual with no credit history, along with fabricated details like a name and address. This synthetic identity is then used to apply for credit cards, loans, or other financial products, often without detection. Because the identity is not linked to any single individual initially, synthetic identity theft can go undetected for long periods, causing significant damage to the individual or organization involved once discovered. For organizations, particularly financial institutions, implementing advanced identity verification processes, such as cross-referencing applicant information against multiple databases, can help identify inconsistencies and detect synthetic identities. Leveraging biometric technologies and advanced fraud detection software, as described in previous sections, enhances the ability to identify and mitigate these risks effectively.

Protecting against identity theft requires organizations to adopt a multi-layered approach that incorporates both technology and human vigilance. One critical aspect is the proper handling and storage of personal information. Organizations must ensure that sensitive data is stored securely using encrypted databases, as discussed earlier, and that only authorized personnel have access to this information. Implementing multi-factor authentication (MFA) systems adds an additional layer of security, requiring employees to verify their identity through multiple methods, such as passwords and biometric scans, before accessing sensitive data. This reduces the likelihood of unauthorized access, even if one layer of protection is compromised. Regular security audits and system updates are also crucial in maintaining data integrity and ensuring that any potential vulnerabilities are addressed promptly.

In addition to securing internal systems, organizations must remain aware of external threats such as phishing scams and social engineering tactics. Identity thieves often employ these methods to trick individuals into revealing their personal information or credentials. Training employees to recognize suspicious communications and establishing clear protocols for reporting such incidents can significantly reduce the risk of a successful attack. Organizations should also educate their customers on the importance of protecting their personal information and advise them on how to identify fraudulent communications. For example, informing customers that the organization will never request sensitive information, such as passwords or Social Security numbers, via email or phone helps build awareness and reduces the likelihood of falling victim to scams.

Another critical element of protecting against identity theft is establishing comprehensive data breach response plans. Despite all precautionary measures, data breaches may still occur, and organizations must be prepared to respond quickly and effectively. A well-structured response plan should include immediate steps for containing the breach, assessing the extent of the damage, notifying affected individuals, and implementing corrective measures to prevent future incidents. Clear communication with those affected is essential to help them take action to protect their identities, such as monitoring their credit reports or placing fraud alerts with credit bureaus. By having a data breach response plan in place, organizations demonstrate their commitment to protecting personal information and minimizing the impact of any potential security breaches.

A proactive approach to identity theft prevention also involves staying up to date with the latest technological developments and best practices in ID verification and data protection. Identity theft tactics continue to evolve, making it essential for organizations to invest in advanced technologies like artificial intelligence (AI) and machine learning for fraud detection. These technologies can analyze vast amounts of data in real-time, identifying patterns or anomalies that might indicate fraudulent activity. For instance, AI systems can flag attempts to open multiple accounts with the same Social Security number but different names or addresses, alerting organizations to possible identity theft. As explored in previous sections on leveraging technology for ID verification, integrating AI and machine learning into the verification process not only enhances security but also improves the efficiency and accuracy of detecting identity fraud.

Legal compliance is another important aspect of protecting against identity theft. Organizations must adhere to both federal and state regulations designed to protect personal information and prevent identity theft. As discussed in earlier sections, the Real ID Act and other federal laws set standards for verifying identities and securing personal information. Compliance with these regulations is essential for organizations to minimize legal risks and ensure that their ID verification processes meet national security standards. State-level laws, such as California's Consumer Privacy Act (CCPA) and the New York SHIELD Act, impose additional requirements for data protection and provide guidelines for responding to breaches. Understanding and adhering to these regulations help organizations maintain compliance and demonstrate their commitment to identity protection.

Another preventive measure is monitoring the dark web for stolen data. Criminals often sell or trade stolen information on the dark web, where it can be used to commit identity theft. Organizations can partner with cybersecurity firms that specialize in monitoring the dark web for signs of compromised data. By proactively searching for leaked information, organizations can take steps to mitigate the damage before criminals have the opportunity to use it. This may involve notifying affected individuals, enhancing security measures, or taking legal action to remove stolen data from illegal marketplaces.

Ultimately, protecting against identity theft is a continuous process that requires vigilance, technological investment, and a commitment to best practices. Organizations must adopt a culture of security and privacy that permeates every aspect of their operations, from the collection and storage of personal information to the training of employees and the maintenance of secure systems. By implementing a comprehensive approach that combines the latest technologies, strict regulatory compliance, and ongoing education, organizations can create a robust defense against identity theft, ensuring that personal information is protected and that the integrity of the ID verification process is maintained. This proactive stance not only mitigates the risk of identity theft but also reinforces the trust and confidence that individuals place in the systems designed to protect their identities.

LEGAL LIMITS OF ID RETENTION AND DATA USE

The legal limits surrounding the retention and use of ID data are crucial for organizations involved in identity verification. Ensuring compliance with these regulations is essential for protecting the privacy of individuals and maintaining the integrity of data handling practices. The laws governing ID retention and data use vary significantly across federal and state levels, and understanding these distinctions is necessary for avoiding legal risks and potential penalties. In many cases, organizations are required to balance the need for ID retention with the obligation to protect individuals' privacy and prevent the misuse of sensitive data. This complex landscape underscores the importance of establishing clear policies and protocols that adhere to legal standards while also prioritizing security and ethical considerations.

At the federal level, several laws establish guidelines for the retention and use of personal data obtained through ID verification processes. The Fair Credit Reporting Act (FCRA) is one example of legislation that governs the use of personal data by entities like credit reporting agencies, employers, and others involved in financial or background checks. The FCRA mandates that personal information must be used for legitimate purposes, such as evaluating creditworthiness or verifying identity, and sets limitations on how long this data can be retained. Organizations that handle ID verification must ensure they are compliant with the FCRA by limiting access to data only to those who have a legitimate need and by securely disposing of the information when it is no longer required. Furthermore, as mentioned in the section on financial ID verification, understanding the requirements of the FCRA helps businesses operate within the bounds of the law while safeguarding the rights of consumers.

Another important federal law is the Gramm-Leach-Bliley Act (GLBA), which imposes data privacy requirements on financial institutions and other entities that handle personal financial information. The GLBA obligates these organizations to develop and implement policies for securely managing personal data, including guidelines on how long such data can be retained. Organizations are required to disclose their information-sharing practices to customers and provide options for opting out of certain uses. This transparency ensures that customers are aware of how their information is being handled, and it aligns with previous sections on the importance of informed consent in ID verification processes. For businesses, maintaining compliance with the GLBA is crucial, as violations can result in severe penalties, including fines and reputational damage.

Healthcare entities must adhere to the Health Insurance Portability and Accountability Act (HIPAA), which outlines strict rules for the retention and use of patient information. HIPAA requires that healthcare providers and related organizations limit access to patient information and protect it through secure systems. The retention period for patient information is regulated under HIPAA, with specific requirements depending on the state in which the healthcare provider operates. This is significant for organizations handling medical IDs and verifying patient identities, as they must ensure compliance with HIPAA to avoid legal repercussions and maintain the trust of their patients. Additionally, as noted in previous sections, the integration of biometric technology in healthcare ID verification processes must align with HIPAA's requirements to ensure that sensitive biometric data, such as fingerprints or facial recognition information, is stored and used appropriately.

State-level laws also play a critical role in determining the legal limits of ID retention and data use, and these laws often complement or expand upon federal regulations. For instance, the California Consumer Privacy Act (CCPA) establishes stringent requirements for businesses that collect and use personal information from California residents. The CCPA mandates that businesses disclose what data they collect, how it is used, and for how long it is retained. It also grants individuals the right to request the deletion of their information and the right to opt out of the sale of their data. Businesses must comply with these requirements by implementing clear policies and procedures for data retention and deletion, ensuring they provide a transparent and compliant framework for managing personal information. As discussed earlier, understanding state-specific regulations like the CCPA is vital for organizations that operate in multiple jurisdictions, as compliance requirements can vary significantly.

In New York, the SHIELD Act requires businesses to implement reasonable safeguards for protecting personal information, including setting retention limits and ensuring secure disposal methods. The act emphasizes the importance of maintaining up-to-date security measures and regularly assessing risks to protect data throughout its lifecycle. The SHIELD Act's requirements are particularly relevant for organizations involved in ID verification, as they must establish comprehensive strategies for managing personal information that comply with both the state law and any applicable federal regulations. The SHIELD Act's focus on secure disposal also aligns with previous sections on the importance of minimizing data retention to reduce the risk of exposure. By securely deleting data when it is no longer necessary, businesses can limit potential points of vulnerability that could be exploited by cybercriminals.

Texas has its own regulations governing ID retention and data use, especially regarding biometric data. The Texas Biometric Privacy Act regulates the collection, storage, and retention of biometric identifiers, such as fingerprints and facial scans. Under this act, entities must obtain informed consent from individuals before collecting biometric data, disclose the specific purpose of the data collection, and establish a retention schedule that limits the storage period to the minimum necessary to achieve that purpose. Once the purpose is fulfilled, the data must be securely deleted. These regulations underscore the importance of transparency and accountability, as businesses must clearly communicate their practices and ensure they comply with state guidelines. For organizations using biometric technology in ID verification, this means integrating practices that not only secure biometric data but also manage it in accordance with legal requirements.

Illinois has also taken a strict approach to the management of biometric data through its Biometric Information Privacy Act (BIPA). BIPA mandates that organizations collect and retain biometric data only after obtaining written consent and providing individuals with information about the purpose and duration of the retention period. BIPA also grants individuals the right to take legal action if their biometric information is mishandled or if businesses fail to comply with the act's requirements. This legal framework serves as a cautionary example for other states, as it demonstrates the importance of adhering to regulations that protect sensitive data. For businesses, BIPA compliance means not only securing the data but also having clear documentation and policies that outline the collection, use, and retention of biometric identifiers. This aligns with previous sections on the importance of informed consent and data transparency in building consumer trust and protecting sensitive information.

Florida's privacy regulations also emphasize the secure management of personal information, particularly in sectors like financial services and healthcare. The state requires organizations to follow strict protocols for data retention and disposal, ensuring that personal data is only kept for as long as necessary to fulfill the purpose for which it was collected. After the data's use is complete, Florida law mandates secure disposal methods to prevent unauthorized access. This regulation reinforces the importance of limiting the storage period of sensitive information and ensuring that data is managed responsibly throughout its lifecycle.

When discussing the legal limits of ID retention and data use, it is crucial to emphasize the principle of data minimization, which is a key aspect of many federal and state privacy regulations. Data minimization involves collecting only the information that is absolutely necessary for the specific purpose of verification or service provision and retaining it only for as long as is legally required or operationally necessary. This approach reduces the amount of data an organization holds at any given time, thereby minimizing the potential impact of a data breach. For organizations, implementing data minimization policies means regularly reviewing the types of data collected during ID verification processes, assessing the necessity of each data point, and securely disposing of any information that exceeds these requirements.

The legal landscape also requires businesses to adopt proper data access controls, ensuring that only authorized personnel can view or use sensitive information. Access controls must be robust, involving multi-factor authentication systems and secure logging of access attempts to create accountability. For instance, in industries like healthcare, where access to patient records is often necessary for medical professionals, limiting access to only those directly involved in the patient's care is essential for compliance with HIPAA and other regulations. Such practices not only protect the individual's privacy but also reduce the likelihood of data being misused for unauthorized purposes. This emphasis on controlled access was previously highlighted in sections on secure digital systems and the use of biometric verification technologies to authenticate authorized personnel securely.

Navigating the legal limits of ID retention and data use involves understanding and complying with a wide array of federal and state regulations. These laws are designed to protect individual privacy and ensure that organizations use and retain data responsibly. Businesses and entities involved in ID verification must be proactive in establishing compliant practices that include data minimization, informed consent, secure storage, and proper disposal methods. Moreover, they must stay informed about evolving legislation, as state laws like the CCPA and BIPA set precedents that could influence regulations across the country. By implementing comprehensive strategies that integrate these legal requirements into their ID verification processes, organizations can protect personal data, maintain regulatory compliance, and uphold the integrity of the information they manage.

WHAT YOU SHOULD DO IF YOUR IDENTITY GETS STOLEN

When your identity is stolen, it can feel like the foundation of your personal and financial security has been ripped away. In today's interconnected world, the risk of identity theft is higher than ever, especially as so much personal information is stored and shared digitally. If your identity has been compromised, the first step is to act quickly, stay calm, and take the right steps to minimize the damage. It is essential to remember that identity theft isn't a single event but an ongoing process. A thief could misuse your information today, next month, or even years down the line, which is why it's vital to understand the long-term implications and manage the situation proactively.

The first action you should take when you realize your identity has been stolen is to confirm the scope of the theft. This involves reviewing your financial accounts, credit reports, and any suspicious activity that may give you a clue about what specific aspects of your identity have been compromised. It could be that only your credit card number was stolen, or it could be more severe, such as the misuse of your Social Security number. In the event of credit card fraud, the process may be more straightforward since most banks have protocols in place to handle these cases. However, if sensitive information like your Social Security number is stolen, the repercussions can be much broader, and you'll need to be even more vigilant.

Once you understand the scale of the theft, it's critical to report the incident to the necessary authorities. Filing a report with the Federal Trade Commission (FTC) is an important first step. The FTC can guide you through the process of managing the theft, and they provide resources and templates for writing letters to creditors, credit bureaus, and other relevant institutions. They will also generate a recovery plan, which can serve as your roadmap throughout this process. In cases involving your Social Security number, it's advisable to reach out to the Social Security Administration as well to inform them of the theft and seek guidance on securing your account.

Contacting the credit bureaus—Equifax, Experian, and TransUnion—is another critical step. You should request a fraud alert or consider freezing your credit. A fraud alert will notify potential lenders that your identity may have been stolen, and they must take extra steps to verify your identity before granting credit in your name. A credit freeze, on the other hand, restricts access to your credit report altogether, preventing new accounts from being opened. While a freeze doesn't impact your credit score, it makes it far more difficult for a thief to open lines of credit using your information. Both of these options provide additional layers of protection, and in some cases, freezing your credit is the stronger option, especially if the theft is more extensive.

Simultaneously, it's crucial to alert your financial institutions and creditors of the theft. Many banks and credit card companies have dedicated fraud departments that handle identity theft cases. They can monitor your accounts for unusual activity, freeze or close compromised accounts, and work with you to reverse fraudulent transactions. Keeping a detailed log of your communications with financial institutions is essential. Document every phone call, email, or letter you send, as you may need this information for future disputes or claims. Ensure that you follow up on any actions or promises made by your bank or creditors, as identity theft recovery often requires persistent effort.

A vital but often overlooked step is to file a police report. While local law enforcement may not always investigate identity theft cases, having a police report on file is important because it can serve as an official document that proves the crime occurred. This report can be useful when dealing with creditors, credit bureaus, or even insurance companies if applicable. In many instances, a police report is necessary for disputing fraudulent accounts or transactions, especially if the identity theft leads to more significant crimes such as tax fraud or false unemployment claims in your name.

As mentioned in a previous section, state-issued identification is also highly vulnerable to identity theft. If your driver's license or state ID was stolen, you should immediately notify the Department of Motor Vehicles (DMV). Some identity thieves may use stolen identification to commit traffic violations or other crimes, which could lead to criminal charges being filed in your name. The DMV can issue a replacement ID and flag your old one as compromised. In some states, they can also issue an entirely new license number, which further protects you from the thief's misuse of your ID. Similar to reporting stolen financial information, make sure to document your communication with the DMV and keep copies of all correspondence.

Tax-related identity theft is another significant concern, particularly if your Social Security number has been compromised. Thieves may attempt to file fraudulent tax returns in your name to claim refunds. If this happens, it is critical to contact the IRS as soon as possible. The IRS can place a hold on your account to prevent further fraudulent activity and assist you in filing an identity theft affidavit. This process may take time, as the IRS has specific procedures for handling identity theft cases, but it is essential to address this issue promptly to avoid further complications. Additionally, consider signing up for an Identity Protection PIN (IP PIN) through the IRS, which is a unique code that will help protect your future tax filings.

Another area of concern that could arise from identity theft is medical fraud. If an identity thief uses your personal information to access healthcare services, it could result in inaccurate medical records, incorrect charges, and even the theft of your health insurance benefits. To prevent this, contact your health insurance provider and request copies of your medical records to review for any discrepancies. If fraudulent activity is detected, report it to your insurer and the U.S. Department of Health and Human Services Office for Civil Rights. This type of fraud can be particularly dangerous, as it may impact your ability to receive proper medical care if false information is included in your medical history.

Identity theft recovery is not a quick process, and staying organized and proactive is critical. Keeping track of all documents, emails, and communication can help you navigate the various agencies and companies involved. Some victims of identity theft may also consider hiring an identity theft protection service to monitor their credit and personal information, although this is a personal choice depending on the complexity of the situation.

Remember that identity theft can have long-lasting effects, and it may take months or even years to fully recover from its impact. By taking swift action, working closely with relevant authorities and institutions, and staying vigilant about your financial and personal information, you can reduce the damage and regain control over your identity.

CHAPTER 12

ETHICAL CONSIDERATIONS IN ID CHECKING

AVOIDING DISCRIMINATION AND PROFILING

In the realm of ID verification, it is crucial to remain conscious of the delicate balance between securing accurate identification and avoiding discriminatory practices or profiling. While the responsibility of verifying identification documents is a necessary part of many industries and settings, it is equally important to conduct this process fairly and without bias. The risk of inadvertently engaging in discrimination or profiling can arise from assumptions about a person's race, ethnicity, gender, age, or socioeconomic background. Preventing such missteps requires a clear understanding of both the legal requirements of ID verification and the ethical standards that must guide your interactions with individuals.

To avoid discrimination, it is essential to apply consistent procedures across all interactions, regardless of the individual being assessed. ID verification should focus solely on the authenticity of the presented document and not on any subjective judgments about the individual presenting it. When examining a state-issued ID, for example, the focus should be on ensuring the information matches the person in front of you, without allowing personal biases to influence the process. This consistency is key in avoiding accusations of unfair treatment or targeting. By creating and following a standardized verification protocol, not only can you mitigate the risk of profiling, but you also contribute to a culture of fairness and respect in all ID-related interactions.

In many cases, discrimination in ID verification can stem from unconscious biases, which may influence decisions without a person even realizing it. These biases can result in one group of people being scrutinized more heavily than others, even when there is no legitimate reason for doing so. For example, individuals from minority ethnic backgrounds or non-native English speakers may experience disproportionate questioning about their IDs, while others might pass through without issue. In a previous section, we discussed the importance of accuracy and diligence in ID checking to prevent fraud, but it is equally important that this diligence is applied uniformly. If some individuals feel they are being treated differently because of their appearance or background, the fairness of the verification process is compromised.

One of the primary ways to avoid discrimination is to rely on objective criteria that are directly related to the ID in question. For instance, when examining an ID, consider the document's features—such as holograms, watermarks, and expiration dates—rather than focusing on the individual's personal characteristics. By keeping the verification process grounded in factual evidence rather than assumptions, you are less likely to engage in profiling. For instance, if an ID appears valid and all the security features check out, there should be no reason to question the individual presenting it more rigorously based solely on their accent or appearance. Remaining objective and adhering to established verification standards will help ensure that each individual is treated equitably.

It is important to remember that discriminatory practices in ID verification can also have serious legal consequences. Various anti-discrimination laws at the federal and state levels, such as the Civil Rights Act, prohibit discrimination based on race, ethnicity, gender, or other protected characteristics. If a person feels they have been discriminated against during an ID verification process, they could potentially file a lawsuit or lodge a formal complaint with the relevant authorities. Therefore, being aware of the legal landscape surrounding discrimination is essential for anyone responsible for ID verification. Following clear guidelines and making sure these guidelines are well communicated to all employees involved in the verification process can help protect against legal challenges.

Moreover, cultural sensitivity and awareness are crucial components of fair and non-discriminatory ID verification. Different cultural norms may influence how individuals present themselves or interact with authority figures during the verification process. Being attuned to these differences without making assumptions is important for fostering trust and avoiding misunderstandings. For example, in some cultures, it may be customary to avoid direct eye contact or to be less verbally assertive, which could be misinterpreted as evasiveness. Rather than jumping to conclusions about a person's behavior, it is important to remain patient, professional, and focused on the task of verifying the ID itself.

Communication plays a significant role in preventing discrimination and profiling. Clear and respectful communication with individuals presenting their IDs is essential. If additional information is required to verify the authenticity of an ID, it is important to explain the situation calmly and professionally, without making the person feel singled out or accused of wrongdoing. Explaining the steps of the verification process transparently can also help alleviate any potential discomfort or confusion the individual might feel. This fosters an environment of respect and reduces the likelihood that individuals will perceive the process as unfair or discriminatory.

At times, ID verification processes may require further scrutiny, particularly if an ID appears to be tampered with or fraudulent. However, it is crucial that this extra scrutiny is based solely on the objective signs of document fraud, as discussed earlier, rather than the individual's personal characteristics. If there is reason to question the legitimacy of an ID, ensure that the process for handling such situations is clearly outlined and applied equally in all cases. This reduces the risk of profiling and ensures that any additional questioning or follow-up is conducted in a fair and consistent manner. In this context, referring to your established protocols, as previously discussed in sections covering proper handling of suspicious documents, can help guide the process and maintain consistency.

Additionally, technology can play an important role in reducing the risk of discrimination during ID verification. Automated systems for scanning IDs, for example, remove much of the subjective element from the process by analyzing the document's security features and alerting the verifier to potential issues. These systems do not rely on human judgment and, as a result, are less likely to be influenced by unconscious biases. However, it is important to remember that even with technology, human oversight is still necessary. Therefore, training employees to understand both the limitations and strengths of these tools is vital in ensuring that their use enhances fairness rather than inadvertently introducing new forms of bias.

Finally, an integral part of avoiding discrimination and profiling in ID verification is ongoing education and training. Employees involved in verifying IDs must be well-trained not only in the technical aspects of document checking but also in recognizing and addressing their own biases. Regular training on cultural sensitivity, anti-discrimination laws, and the ethical responsibilities of ID verifiers can help maintain a professional and impartial approach. Such training should be mandatory and periodically refreshed to ensure that everyone involved in the process remains aware of the importance of fairness and equality.

Avoiding discrimination and profiling in ID verification requires a commitment to fairness, consistency, and objectivity. By focusing solely on the validity of the documents and applying uniform standards to all individuals, ID verifiers can ensure that the process is both effective and ethical. Remaining aware of the potential for unconscious bias, adhering to legal requirements, and fostering clear communication can further reduce the risks of unfair treatment. In doing so, the integrity of the ID verification process is upheld, and individuals can have confidence that they are being treated with respect and impartiality.

BALANCING SECURITY AND CUSTOMER EXPERIENCE

In any environment where identity verification is necessary, whether it be for financial services, retail, or entry into secure locations, a crucial balance must be struck between maintaining security and providing a smooth, respectful customer experience. Security, in the context of ID verification, is essential for protecting against fraud, identity theft, and unauthorized access. However, if the verification process is overly complicated or invasive, it risks alienating customers and damaging their trust in your organization. Striking this balance requires a well-thought-out approach that ensures safety without sacrificing the efficiency and comfort that customers expect.

A key component of this balance lies in the design and implementation of the verification process. On one hand, robust security measures are necessary to detect and prevent fraudulent IDs or documents. As discussed earlier, ID verification involves the careful inspection of key security features on state-issued IDs, including holograms, watermarks, and microprinting. However, while such thoroughness is necessary for ensuring the authenticity of the documents, the process must not be so intrusive that it makes customers feel distrusted or uncomfortable. Customers often expect a fast and seamless experience, and delays caused by overzealous verification efforts can lead to frustration and dissatisfaction. Ensuring that the ID verification process is streamlined and efficient, while still maintaining the highest standards of security, is essential for creating a positive interaction.

Technology can play a pivotal role in achieving this balance between security and customer experience. Automated ID scanners and verification systems have become increasingly popular tools in many industries, allowing for quick and accurate analysis of identification documents. These systems minimize the need for manual inspection, reducing the chances of human error while also speeding up the process. By implementing technology that can verify IDs in a matter of seconds, businesses can enhance security without sacrificing customer satisfaction. However, it is important that these technological solutions are implemented thoughtfully, as even advanced systems can introduce challenges if they are not user-friendly. Customers may feel uneasy if the technology fails or if they perceive it to be unnecessarily complicated. Therefore, investing in technology that is both reliable and easy to use is crucial.

Another factor that influences the balance between security and customer experience is the way employees interact with customers during the ID verification process. Even when security protocols demand a detailed inspection of an ID, the manner in which this is communicated to the customer can make a significant difference. Clear, polite, and respectful communication helps customers understand the importance of the process without feeling like they are being scrutinized or inconvenienced. Employees should be trained not only in the technical aspects of ID verification but also in customer service techniques that ensure interactions remain positive, even in situations where additional verification steps are necessary. This aligns with earlier sections about avoiding discrimination and profiling, where we emphasized the importance of consistent, respectful treatment for all individuals. Ensuring that employees engage customers with a professional and courteous demeanor will help maintain a positive experience while still adhering to security protocols.

Building trust with customers is another critical aspect of balancing security with customer experience. Customers need to feel confident that their personal information is being handled with care and that the verification process is necessary for their protection. Providing transparency around why ID checks are conducted and how the process benefits the customer can help build this trust. When customers understand that the measures in place are there to protect them from fraud or identity theft, they are more likely to appreciate the security protocols rather than view them as an inconvenience. This is particularly important in situations where more thorough checks are required, such as in financial transactions or access to restricted areas. Educating customers on the purpose of these measures, while ensuring that their information is handled securely, fosters trust and strengthens the overall relationship between the customer and the business.

It is also important to consider that not all customers will have the same level of familiarity with the ID verification process. For some, it may be a routine part of their experience, while for others, it may be an unfamiliar or even stressful interaction. This is particularly true in scenarios where ID verification involves sensitive situations, such as age-restricted purchases or high-security environments. In these cases, a more personalized approach may be needed to ensure that the process does not feel intimidating or overly intrusive. Taking the time to explain the steps in a clear and supportive manner can go a long way in ensuring that customers feel comfortable, even when additional verification steps are necessary. This approach also ties into the broader need for cultural sensitivity, as discussed in earlier sections, where we noted the importance of being aware of how cultural backgrounds can influence individuals' perceptions of authority and identification processes.

A smooth customer experience also depends on minimizing the friction caused by errors or discrepancies in the verification process. For instance, if an ID is expired or contains incorrect information, it is important that the issue is handled efficiently and professionally. Customers should not be made to feel at fault for such issues, especially if they are unaware of the problem. Offering solutions, such as explaining the steps to update an ID or providing alternative verification options, can help mitigate any negative feelings that may arise from a failed ID check. The key is to address the situation without creating unnecessary stress or frustration for the customer. In some cases, businesses may have policies in place that allow for secondary forms of identification to be accepted in the event of a discrepancy, and it is important that employees are well-versed in these procedures to ensure a seamless experience.

At the same time, security should never be compromised in the name of convenience. While it may be tempting to streamline the verification process by cutting corners, doing so can open the door to fraud and other security risks. The goal is to create a verification process that is both efficient and effective. In high-security environments or industries where compliance with strict regulations is required, such as in banking or government services, the stakes are even higher. In these situations, maintaining the integrity of the ID verification process is paramount, but it is still possible to do so in a way that respects the customer's time and comfort. As with any security measure, it is important to strike a balance where neither security nor customer satisfaction is compromised.

Moreover, businesses must regularly evaluate and adjust their ID verification processes to ensure that they are keeping pace with both technological advancements and evolving customer expectations. The needs of customers today are different from those of a decade ago, and the expectations around speed, convenience, and security continue to evolve. As discussed in earlier sections, the rise of digital ID verification options and other technological innovations are changing the landscape of identity verification. Businesses must remain adaptable, finding ways to integrate new technologies that enhance both security and customer experience without creating unnecessary barriers. This may involve implementing new software, updating training programs, or revising policies to reflect current best practices.

Ultimately, balancing security with customer experience requires a holistic approach that prioritizes both safety and satisfaction. By implementing efficient verification processes, investing in user-friendly technology, training employees in both technical and customer service skills, and fostering clear communication, businesses can create an environment where security measures are respected and appreciated by customers. This balance not only protects against fraud and other risks but also builds lasting trust and loyalty among customers, ensuring that they feel valued and protected throughout their experience.

CONCLUSION

As we draw to a close, it is important to reflect on the key insights explored throughout the course of this guide. ID verification remains one of the most vital aspects of maintaining security, preventing fraud, and ensuring that businesses and institutions uphold both the integrity of their operations and the safety of those they serve. The complexities of this process extend far beyond simply checking whether an ID looks legitimate. Instead, it involves a multifaceted understanding of security features, legal obligations, and ethical considerations that collectively form a comprehensive approach to identity verification.

One of the most important elements that has been emphasized is the need for accuracy in every step of the ID verification process. Whether you are working with a state-issued driver's license, a passport, or any other form of government identification, a deep understanding of the various security features embedded within these documents is crucial. From holograms and UV elements to microprinting and embedded chips, each of these components plays a role in establishing the authenticity of an ID. Being able to identify these features confidently reduces the risk of falling victim to sophisticated forgery techniques. As discussed in earlier sections, individuals tasked with verifying IDs must remain vigilant and knowledgeable in detecting even the smallest signs of tampering or alteration. This diligence is not only about preventing financial loss or security breaches but also about safeguarding the reputation and trust of the institutions that rely on these systems.

Equally important is the role of consistency in the ID verification process. Consistency ensures that every individual is subjected to the same level of scrutiny and that the process is applied uniformly across all interactions. This not only strengthens the overall effectiveness of identity verification but also plays a significant role in ensuring that the process is fair and unbiased. Earlier, we examined the dangers of discrimination and profiling, highlighting the importance of applying the same standards to all individuals, regardless of their background or appearance. When a consistent approach is followed, it becomes easier to avoid unnecessary assumptions that could lead to biased treatment. By adhering to a uniform set of procedures, you mitigate the risks of allowing personal bias to influence your decisions, ensuring that fairness remains a cornerstone of the verification process.

Another critical point that has been addressed throughout the guide is the evolving role of technology in ID verification. The rise of automated systems, facial recognition software, and digital identity verification solutions has transformed the way businesses and institutions approach the process. While these technological advancements offer significant advantages in terms of speed, accuracy, and fraud detection, it is equally important to recognize that technology must be used thoughtfully and responsibly. As we have seen in earlier sections, relying solely on technology without human oversight can lead to issues, such as system malfunctions or inaccuracies that may negatively impact the customer experience. A hybrid approach, combining the power of technology with human judgment, allows for the best of both worlds. This ensures that the verification process remains both secure and adaptable to varying situations, while still providing a personalized touch when necessary.

Balancing security and customer experience has also been a recurring theme throughout the guide. It is clear that while security must always be a top priority, the way it is enforced can significantly impact how customers perceive the process. When ID verification is handled efficiently, respectfully, and with clear communication, customers are more likely to view it as a necessary and valuable part of the interaction. In contrast, when the process feels overly invasive or disorganized, it can lead to frustration and damage the relationship between the customer and the business. We have explored the importance of training employees not only in the technical aspects of ID verification but also in customer service, so they can effectively manage these interactions while maintaining security. The trust that is built during these moments plays a key role in creating a positive customer experience, and it reinforces the legitimacy of the security measures in place.

Another essential element of this guide has been the legal framework surrounding ID verification. Legal compliance is a non-negotiable part of the verification process, as it ensures that the rights of individuals are protected while businesses meet their regulatory obligations. Various federal and state laws govern the use of ID verification, particularly when it comes to privacy, discrimination, and recordkeeping. Understanding these laws is fundamental for anyone involved in the process, as violations can lead to serious consequences, both in terms of legal penalties and reputational damage. Earlier, we discussed the importance of maintaining a delicate balance between thorough verification and respecting customer privacy. By adhering to these legal requirements, businesses can protect themselves from potential liabilities while upholding the ethical standards expected in today's environment.

As we look toward the future of ID verification, it is clear that the landscape will continue to evolve. With new technologies emerging, such as blockchain-based digital identities, biometric verification, and artificial intelligence, the way we authenticate identity is poised to become even more secure and streamlined. However, the core principles of accuracy, consistency, and fairness will remain constant. Regardless of the tools and methods used, these guiding principles will continue to be the foundation upon which effective ID verification is built. Staying informed about these innovations and adapting to new methods will be essential for keeping pace with evolving threats and maintaining the integrity of the verification process.

The challenges faced in the ID verification process are not static; they are continuously shifting as fraudsters find new ways to exploit weaknesses and as regulatory standards evolve. Therefore, ongoing education and training are paramount for staying ahead of these challenges. As highlighted throughout the guide, the importance of regular training for employees involved in ID verification cannot be overstated. By equipping them with up-to-date knowledge on the latest security features, technologies, and legal standards, you ensure that they remain vigilant and effective in their roles. Additionally, fostering a culture of awareness and adaptability within your organization allows you to respond proactively to new developments, rather than simply reacting to emerging threats.

In conclusion, the journey through the ID verification process is one that requires a commitment to excellence, security, and fairness. By implementing the strategies and best practices outlined throughout the guide, you not only protect your organization from the risks associated with identity fraud and unauthorized access but also create a positive, trustworthy experience for customers. The ultimate goal is to foster an environment where security measures are respected, understood, and seamlessly integrated into the daily operations of your business. By balancing the demands of security with the needs of customers, and by continually staying informed and adapting to new challenges, you set the stage for a secure and successful future in ID verification.

PART 5

Appendices

GLOSSARY OF ID-RELATED TERMS

- ❖ **Access Control**: A security technique that regulates who can view or use resources in a computing environment, often through ID verification.
- ❖ **Authentication**: The process of verifying the identity of a user, device, or other entity in a computer system, typically using credentials like passwords or IDs.
- ❖ **Biometric Authentication**: A method of verifying identity using unique biological characteristics, such as fingerprints, facial recognition, or iris scans.
- ❖ **Chip-Based ID**: An identification card that contains a microchip used to store data and enhance security, often seen in passports and driver's licenses.
- ❖ **Compliance**: Adherence to laws, regulations, and standards governing ID verification, including privacy and anti-fraud regulations.
- ❖ **Counterfeit ID**: A fraudulent or fake identification document created to deceive or impersonate another individual.
- ❖ **Credential**: A documented form of evidence that proves an individual's identity, such as an ID card, passport, or digital certificate.
- ❖ **Customer Due Diligence (CDD)**: A regulatory process involving the verification of customer identity to prevent fraud and comply with anti-money laundering laws.
- ❖ **Data Breach**: An incident where sensitive, protected, or confidential information is accessed or disclosed without authorization, often involving personal ID data.
- ❖ **Digital Identity**: The online or networked representation of an individual's identity, often secured through passwords, biometrics, or digital certificates.
- ❖ **Document Security Features**: Special visual elements such as holograms, UV ink, watermarks, and microprinting used to prevent counterfeiting and fraud in identification documents.
- ❖ **Driver's License**: A state-issued identification card that authorizes an individual to operate a motor vehicle and serves as an official form of ID.

- ❖ **Dual-Factor Authentication (2FA)**: A security process requiring two methods of authentication from separate categories of credentials to verify identity.
- ❖ **Encryption**: A security process that encodes data, including identity information, to prevent unauthorized access during transmission or storage.
- ❖ **Expiration Date**: The date after which an identification document is no longer valid and must be renewed or replaced.
- ❖ **Facial Recognition**: A biometric technology that uses the unique features of a person's face to verify their identity.
- ❖ **Fake ID**: A forged or altered identification document used to deceive or misrepresent one's age or identity.
- ❖ **Fraud Detection**: Techniques and technologies used to identify fraudulent activities, including the use of counterfeit or stolen IDs.
- ❖ **Hologram**: A 3D image embedded in identification documents as a security feature to prevent counterfeiting.
- ❖ **Identity Fraud**: The unauthorized use of another person's personal information, such as their name, ID, or Social Security number, for deceptive purposes.
- ❖ **Identity Theft**: The illegal act of obtaining and using someone else's personal identification information for fraud or criminal activity.
- ❖ **Issuer**: The entity, such as a government agency or organization, responsible for creating and distributing identification documents.
- ❖ **Magnetic Stripe**: A band of magnetic material on the back of ID cards, like credit cards or driver's licenses, that stores information.
- ❖ **Microprinting**: Extremely small text or images on an identification document, used as a security feature to prevent counterfeiting.
- ❖ **National ID**: A government-issued document used to verify the identity and nationality of an individual within a country.
- ❖ **OCR (Optical Character Recognition)**: Technology that converts different types of documents, such as scanned paper documents or ID cards, into editable and searchable data.
- ❖ **Passport**: A government-issued document that certifies the holder's identity and nationality, used primarily for international travel.
- ❖ **Personally Identifiable Information (PII)**: Data that can be used to identify an individual, such as name, address, Social Security number, and ID number.

- ❖ **Phishing**: A type of cyberattack that attempts to steal sensitive information, such as ID numbers or passwords, by disguising as a trustworthy entity.
- ❖ **Proof of Identity**: Documentation or evidence required to verify an individual's identity, such as an ID card or birth certificate.
- ❖ **QR Code**: A machine-readable code often found on ID documents that stores information about the cardholder and can be scanned for verification.
- ❖ **Radio Frequency Identification (RFID)**: Technology used in ID cards that allows data to be transmitted wirelessly, commonly found in passports and access cards.
- ❖ **Real ID Act**: A U.S. federal law passed in 2005 that sets standards for the issuance of sources of identification, such as driver's licenses and state ID cards.
- ❖ **Record Keeping**: The process of storing and maintaining records of identity verifications, often required for compliance with laws and regulations.
- ❖ **Resident Alien Card (Green Card)**: A U.S. ID card issued to non-citizens that proves lawful permanent residency.
- ❖ **Scalability**: The capacity of ID verification systems to handle increasing numbers of verifications as a business or institution grows.
- ❖ **Secure Element**: A dedicated hardware component, such as a chip, used to store sensitive information securely on an ID document.
- ❖ **Smart Card**: A type of ID card with embedded integrated circuits that can process information and enhance security during verification.
- ❖ **Social Security Number (SSN)**: A unique identification number issued to U.S. citizens and residents used primarily for taxation and Social Security benefits but often used as a key identifier.
- ❖ **Watermark**: A security feature in identification documents, visible when held up to the light, used to deter counterfeiting.

LIST OF STATE DMV WEBSITES AND CONTACT INFORMATION

Here's a state-by-state list of DMV websites and contact information for the USA:

Alabama
- Website: (https://revenue.alabama.gov/motor-vehicle/)
- Phone: (334) 242-9000

Alaska
- Website: (http://doa.alaska.gov/dmv/)
- Phone: (855) 269-5551

Arizona
- Website: (https://azdot.gov/motor-vehicles)
- Phone: (602) 255-0072

Arkansas
- Website: (https://www.dfa.arkansas.gov/motor-vehicle)
- Phone: (501) 682-4692

California
- Website: (https://www.dmv.ca.gov)
- Phone: 1-800-777-0133

Colorado
- Website: (https://dmv.colorado.gov/)
- Phone: (303) 205-5600

Connecticut
- Website: (https://portal.ct.gov/dmv)
- Phone: (800) 842-8222

Delaware
- Website: (https://dmv.de.gov/)
- Phone: (302) 744-2500

Florida
- Website: (https://www.flhsmv.gov/)
- Phone: (850) 617-2000

Georgia
- Website: (https://dds.georgia.gov/)
- Phone: (678) 413-8400

Hawaii
- Website: (https://www.hawaiicounty.gov/departments/finance/vehicle-registration-licensing)
- Phone: (808) 961-8351

Idaho
- Website: (https://itd.idaho.gov/dmv/)
- Phone: (208) 334-8000

Illinois
- Website: (https://www.cyberdriveillinois.com)
- Phone: (800) 252-8980

Indiana
- Website: (https://www.in.gov/bmv/)
- Phone: (888) 692-6841

Iowa
- Website: (https://iowadot.gov/mvd)
- Phone: (515) 244-8725

Kansas
- Website: (https://www.ksrevenue.org/dov.html)
- Phone: (785) 296-3621

Kentucky
- Website: (https://drive.ky.gov/)
- Phone: (502) 564-1257

Louisiana
- Website: (https://www.expresslane.org/)
- Phone: (225) 925-6146

Maine
- Website: (https://www.maine.gov/sos/bmv/)
- Phone: (207) 624-9000

Maryland
- Website: (https://mva.maryland.gov/)
- Phone: (410) 768-7000

Massachusetts
- Website: (https://www.mass.gov/orgs/massachusetts-registry-of-motor-vehicles)
- Phone: (857) 368-8000

Michigan
- Website: (https://www.michigan.gov/sos)
- Phone: (888) 767-6424

Minnesota
- Website: (https://dvs.dps.mn.gov/)
- Phone: (651) 297-2126

Mississippi
- Website: (https://www.driverservicebureau.dps.ms.gov/)
- Phone: (601) 987-1212

Missouri
- Website: (https://dor.mo.gov/motor-vehicle/)
- Phone: (573) 751-4509

Montana
- Website: (https://dojmt.gov/driving/)
- Phone: (406) 444-3933

Nebraska
- Website: (https://dmv.nebraska.gov/)
- Phone: (402) 471-3985

Nevada
- Website: (http://www.dmvnv.com/)
- Phone: (775) 684-4368

New Hampshire
- Website: (https://www.nh.gov/safety/divisions/dmv/)
- Phone: (603) 227-4000

New Jersey
- Website: (https://www.state.nj.us/mvc/)
- Phone: (609) 292-6500

New Mexico
- Website: (https://www.mvd.newmexico.gov/)
- Phone: (888) 683-4636

New York
- Website: (https://dmv.ny.gov/)
- Phone: (518) 486-9786

North Carolina
- Website: (https://www.ncdot.gov/dmv/)
- Phone: (919) 715-7000

North Dakota
- Website: (https://www.dot.nd.gov/divisions/mv/mv.htm)
- Phone: (701) 328-2725

Ohio
- Website: (https://bmv.ohio.gov/)

- Phone: (844) 644-6268

Oklahoma
- Website: (https://www.ok.gov/dps/)
- Phone: (405) 425-2424

Oregon
- Website: (https://www.oregon.gov/ODOT/DMV/)
- Phone: (503) 945-5000

Pennsylvania
- Website: (https://www.dmv.pa.gov)
- Phone: (717) 412-5300

Rhode Island
- Website: (http://www.dmv.ri.gov/)
- Phone: (401) 462-4368

South Carolina
- Website: (http://www.scdmvonline.com/)
- Phone: (803) 896-5000

South Dakota
- Website: (https://dps.sd.gov/driver-licensing)
- Phone: (605) 773-6883

Tennessee
- Website: (https://www.tn.gov/safety)
- Phone: (866) 849-3548

Texas
- Website: (https://www.txdmv.gov/)
- Phone: (888) 368-4689

Utah
- Website: (https://dmv.utah.gov/)
- Phone: (801) 297-7780

Vermont
- Website: (https://dmv.vermont.gov/)
- Phone: (802) 828-2000

Virginia
- Website: (https://www.dmv.virginia.gov/)
- Phone: (804) 497-7100

Washington
- Website: (https://www.dol.wa.gov/)
- Phone: (360) 902-3900

West Virginia
- Website: (https://transportation.wv.gov/DMV/)
- Phone: (800) 642-9066

Wisconsin
-         Website: (https://wisconsindot.gov/Pages/online-srvcs/external/dmv.aspx)
- Phone: (608) 264-7447

Wyoming

- Website:
(http://www.dot.state.wy.us/home/driver_license_records.html)

- Phone: (307) 777-4800

SAMPLE STATE ID TEMPLATES

https://www.nationalnotary.org/

https://www.shutterstock.com/search/usa-id-card